D0454492

# Simon & Schuster's
# Guide to
# ORCHIDS

## Alberto Fanfani
## and Walter Rossi

U.S. Editor
Stanley Schuler

A FIRESIDE BOOK
PUBLISHED BY SIMON & SCHUSTER INC.
New York  London  Toronto  Sydney  Tokyo

*To Isa*
*Whose help in resolving initial doubts and difficulties fostered my love for orchids.*

Copyright © 1988 by Arnoldo Mondadori Editore S.p.A., Milan
English translation copyright © 1989 by Arnoldo Mondadori Editore S.p.A., Milan

English translation by John Gilbert

All rights reserved
including the right of reproduction
in whole or in part in any form.

Simon and Schuster/Fireside Books,
Published by Simon & Schuster Inc.
Simon & Schuster Building
Rockefeller Center
1230 Avenue of the Americas
New York, New York 10020

SIMON AND SCHUSTER, FIRESIDE, and colophons are registered trademarks of Simon & Schuster Inc.

Originally published in Italy in 1988 by Arnoldo Mondadori Editore S.p.A., Milan, under the title *Tutto Orchidee*.

Symbols by Adriana Casu
Drawings by Vittorio Salarolo

Printed and bound in Italy
by Officine Grafiche A. Mondadori Editore, Verona

10 9 8 7 6 5 4 3 2 1
10 9 8 7 6 5 4 3 2 1 Pbk.

### Library of Congress Cataloging in Publication Data

Fanfani, Alberto.
  [Tutto orchidee. English]
  Simon & Schuster's guide to orchids / by Alberto Fanfani and
 Walter Rossi : U.S. editor, Stanley Schuler : [English translation
 by John Gilbert].
    p.   cm.
  Translation of: Tutto orchidee,
  Includes index.
  ISBN 0-671-67797-7.   ISBN 0-671-67798-5 (A Fireside book : pbk.)
 1. Orchids. 2. Orchid culture. 3. Orchids--Pictorial works.
 I. Rossi, Walter. II. Schuler, Stanley. III. Title. IV. Title:
 Simon and Schuster's guide to orchids. V. Title: Guide to orchids.
 SB409.F3613 1989
 635.9'3415--dc19                                          88-29797
                                                               CIP

# CONTENTS

KEY TO SYMBOLS                    page 7

INTRODUCTION                     page 9

ENTRIES                       entries 1 - 162

GLOSSARY                        page 247

BIBLIOGRAPHY                     page 249

INDEX                          page 251

# KEY TO SYMBOLS

## CULTIVATION TEMPERATURE

cool house

intermediate or
temperate house

hothouse

## AMOUNT OF LIGHT REQUIRED

full sun

half shade

shade

## SCENT

absent

present

**Note**

The symbols that accompany each individual entry are only intended as a guideline to the cultivation requirements of each species: in fact, certain species have a broad tolerance to surrounding conditions.

For an explanation of "hothouse," "intermediate or temperate house" and "cool house" see page 26 of the introduction.

For easy reference the entries are ordered according to alphabetical sequence, rather than taxonomy, with the sole exception of *Odontocidium* (entry 101), which follows *Odontoglossum* since it is a hybrid of the latter.

Terrestrial species are accompanied by few or no symbols because they are either protected species and consequently must and cannot be collected and cultivated, or they need to be cultivated outdoors and therefore do not need greenhouse treatment.

The family of orchids, one of the most highly evolved of the entire plant kingdom, comprises over 25,000 individual species, with new discoveries being made and described every year. As a result of the wide distribution area, ranging from the Equator to the Arctic Circle, from lowland plains almost up to the snow line in mountain areas, the species vary greatly: they may be terrestrial (growing in ground, as opposed to water), epiphytic (growing above the ground, supported nonparasitically by another plant of object and deriving nutrients and water from the surrounding air), lithophytic (growing on the surface of rocks), or even subterranean (growing beneath the surface of the growing medium).

For thousands of years in every continent man has had direct contact with these plants, obsessed with the beauty of their flowers, attracted by their heavy perfume, or intrigued by the essences that can be extracted from them. In Europe, where cultivation dates back to the ancient civilizations of the Mediterranean, the fathers of orchidology are considered to be the Greek philosopher Theophrastus (372?-287 B.C.) and, much later, the Swedish botanist Carl Linnaeus (1707-78).

It was Theophrastus who first used the Greek word ὄρχις (orchis) to indicate the particular group of plants whose roots, dried and chopped, were used in the traditional pharmacopoeia of Greece and neighboring Asia Minor as antidepressants and stimulants, and even today in some rural areas of these countries "salep," a nutritious drink prepared from the dried tubers of certain orchids, is not uncommonly found. It was not until the mid eighteenth century that the name was applied to the whole family of orchids in Linnaeus' *Species Plantarum*, which marked the beginning of modern plant taxonomy.

However, besides Theophrastus and Linnaeus, many other people were interested in orchids principally as medicinal plants, and this is testified by references in the medical books and herbals of men such as Dioscorides (first century A.D.), Otto Brunfels of Strasbourg (c. 1488-1534), Leonhard Fuchs (1501-66), and John Gerard (1542-1612).

In China some 2,500 years ago, Confucius commended orchids for their wondrous beauty and scent, and the first book on the cultivation of orchids, giving descriptions of species and varieties, was probably written in Chinese in around the year A.D. 1000.

Ancient Aztec inscriptions tell us how the fruit of the tropical climbing orchid genus *Vanilla* was used by early Aztec peoples to flavor a traditional drink made from cocoa beans.

In more recent times, beginning in the early nineteenth century, the sudden surge of interest in the collection of tropical orchids led to the plants frequently being featured in literature, in fiction as well as in science. Examples range from Darwin's treatise on the pollination of orchids by insects to Proust's perverse obsession with the cattleya in *Swann's Way*, from the scientific works of Bernard and others who revealed the secrets of how these plants developed, to the detective stories of Rex Stout and his orchid-raising hero Nero Wolfe.

Until the twentieth century, when the technique of raising orchids in

*Old treetrunk covered by hundreds of orchids in West Africa.*

a greenhouse was transformed by the efforts of Bernard, Knudsen and Morel, the plants hitherto cultivated by the great European collectors with varying degrees of success during the previous 150 years, had all originated from the collections that the famous plant hunters, financed by European enthusiasts, sent or brought back from the intertropical zones of other continents.

The first mention of a tropical orchid to be seen, for a very brief period, in a European greenhouse, was a specimen of *Bletia verecunda*, which was sent from the Bahamas in 1731 by Peter Collinson to a Mr. Wager in England. Evidently eighteenth-century growers had more success with *Epidendrum* and *Vanilla* species, which are mentioned by Miller in his book on floriculture (1768), and with *Phaius tankervilleae* and *Cymbidium ensifolium*, imported in 1778 from China by the English physician John Fothergill 1712-80. By 1794 there were 15 orchid species being cultivated in the Royal Botanic Gardens at Kew, in London, including the now very common *Encyclia cochleata* and *Encyclia fragrans*, both from the West Indies.

Throughout the nineteenth century England remained the principal importer of orchids, followed by Holland and Belgium.

Intrepid plant hunters, wealthy benefactors, astute businessmen, famous scientists, and keen gardeners have all helped to give the orchid international status and their names are linked with those of the flowers they imported and loved: Cattley, Skinner, Bowring, Loddiges, Lindley, Sander, Lobb, Gardner, Veitch, Low, Godefroy, Van Houtte, Vuylsteke, Lawrence, Gould, etc.

11

*Monopodial structure:* Diaphananthe bidens.

The excesses of the early years of the twentieth century outdid even those of the previous century. Crazy prices were paid for single specimens of species originating in places for which there were no records; over-zealous enthusiasts would collect tens of thousands of specimens of an individual species so as to exhaust the source and thus obtain exclusive rights; eccentric wills were made giving instructions to destroy entire collections so that later generations could not benefit from them; and the first hybrids commanded prices that were beyond belief.... All this activity, recorded in books, makes fascinating reading and testifies to a passion which, in other forms, remains unabated even today.

Successful scientific research into the reproduction, planting and cultivation of orchids has now made orchid growing much easier, and what was previously a mania pursued by a few privileged collectors has today been transformed into a hobby for everyone to enjoy.

## STRUCTURE

Orchids, whether grown as botanical species or hybrids, for cut flowers or as a collection, are generally grown in greenhouses of varying size and sophistication. Although occasionally terrestrial, the majority of orchid plants are epiphytes or lithophytes, (i.e. living on other plants or on rocks,) originating from the intertropical regions of the various continents.

The structure of these orchids conforms to two basic models:

monopodial or sympodial. Monopodial orchids are plants that have neither rhizome (modified stem) nor pseudobulbs, and grow from a single vegetative apex (tip). All the Vandeae provide good examples of this type of structure. The stem, of varying length, is swollen, erect or drooping, and may have leaves, well spaced or close together, along its entire length or only near the tip; in the latter case, as a rule, the lower leaves have fallen, so that only their dry, basal portion is left around the stem.

The genus *Vanilla*, whose climbing stems may reach lengths of several hundred feet, also belongs to the group of monopodial orchids. Other monopodial species, usually of small or average dimensions, are devoid of leaves and the roots have a photosynthetic function: typical examples are those belonging to the genera *Microcoelia* and *Chiloschista*. Monopodial orchids sprout new growth by developing axillary shoots that eventually grow into new plants. In many species the roots, which are generally quite thick, round or flattened, are also produced from the aerial part of the stem.

Sympodial orchids grow from a number of vegetative apices situated at varying intervals on the rhizome, which is often much branched. The rhizome is a creeping stem, sometimes underground, which produces other stems, incorrectly called secondary stems, more or less erect, and in some instances almost absent, as in species belonging to the subfamily Cypripedioideae; these may well swell into reserve organs known as pseudobulbs. In the subtribe Pleurothallidinae, such bulb-like structures are often absent.

In sympodial orchids the leaves, which may be produced either at the base, the apex or along the whole length of the pseudobulbs, are deciduous or persistent. The roots are produced from the rhizome. In the genus *Dendrobium*, for example, given particular conditions in the surroundings, new shoots may sprout from the nodes of the pseudobulbs, and new roots will emerge from the base of these shoots. The pseudobulbs of some species of the genus *Maxillaria* grow from a secondary stem that has leaves along its entire length. In the genus *Scaphyglottis* new pseudobulbs may be produced, repeatedly, at the apex of the old ones, but this structure is rare.

The pseudobulbs, which may vary in shape within the same genus, can be extremely small, $\frac{1}{32}$ to $\frac{3}{32}$ in (1–2 mm) in diameter, as in *Bulbophyllum globuliforme* and *B. minutissimum*, or may grow to as much as 16 ft (5 m), as in species such as *Grammatophyllum speciosum* and *G. papuanum*, generally considered to be the giants of the orchid world. The rhizome itself, between one pseudobulb and another, may be very short, so that these organs are necessarily packed closely together, typical examples being *Cymbidium* and *Stanhopea*; in other species the rhizome may be fairly long, in which case the plants are able to put out new growth freely to form often quite large clumps, as in various species of *Cattleya* and *Bulbophyllum*.

**Roots** The main characteristic of the majority of orchids is the presence of a layer of spongy tissue, known as velamen, around the true root. Although not exclusive to this family of plants, the velamen is in this case well developed and present not only in epiphytes and lithophytes but also in terrestrial orchids. This structure, which is more or less developed according to the species, facilitates the absorption of water and mineral salts, especially among the epiphytes. The velamen has also been shown to be highly important for water conservation and protection from strong light.

The vegetative root tip of epiphytic orchids may be exposed to the light and is generally green, for here the chloroplasts are not obscured by the velamen, whereas in certain species that lack leaves photosynthesis is carried out in the entire root structure. In many terrestrial orchids, as in the genus *Paphiopedilum*, root hairs are also to be found.

**Pseudobulbs** These are usually rounded in shape but may also be ovoid, ellipsoid, fusiform, clavate or cylindrical, sometimes elongated so as to be stick-like or compressed either from side to side or from top to bottom. Their surface may be smooth, rough or variously furrowed; and sometimes they may be enfolded by dry bracts, either completely or only around the base.

**Leaves** In the majority of orchids the leaves are distichous, i.e. arranged alternately on opposite sides of the stem; even in those species that are characteristically monopodial (single-stemmed) an examination of the position of the sheaths will reveal this arrangement.

In many species of orchid in which pseudobulbs are absent, the

Chiloschista lunifera, *an orchid that has no leaves.*

*Leaf shape (very simplified): 1, subulate; 2, linear; 3, oblong; 4, elliptic; 5, lanceolate; 6, oblanceolate; 7, ovate; 8, obovate; 9, cordate; 10, triangular; 11, sagittate.*

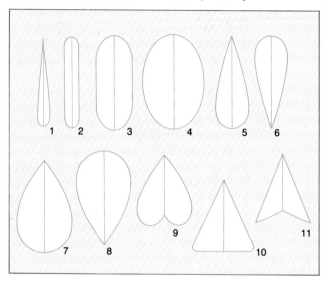

leaves have been transformed into organs for storing food and water. Thus there is a progression from what might be regarded as the initial state, as in various species of *Phalaenopsis*, where the leaves are simply fleshy, through intermediate stages, as in *Dendrobium leonis* and *Angraecum distichum*, culminating in *D. cucumerinum* and *D. linguiforme*, where the leaves are true reserve organs.

The leaves of most orchid plants tend to be coriaceous to some degree, even to the point of resembling card; thinner, membranous leaves are always associated with large or moderately large pseudobulbs. In the majority of cases, given that orchids are monocotyledons, the principal veins run parallel and the interstices are not very prominent. In many species there is a line at the base of the leaves where they tend to break off, whether or not they continue with a basal sheath that encircles the stem or the pseudobulb. Sometimes this abscission zone does not appear at the base of the stalk, as in certain species of the genus *Oeceoclades*. In most instances, the fall of a leaf results in a clear, smooth mark, and sometimes, as in *Catasetum*, this is furnished with spines. Because there are so many species, the leaves take on a wide variety of shapes, the principal types of which are illustrated above.

**Inflorescences** The inflorescences of orchids are produced from the leaf axil or opposite it, at the base of the pseudobulb, at the tip of the stem or from the pseudobulb itself. The typical structure is a raceme, namely a stem or rachis on which single flowers with stalks

*Diagram of the inflorescences: 1, single flower; 2, corymb; 3, umbel; 4, spike; 5, raceme; 6, panicle.*

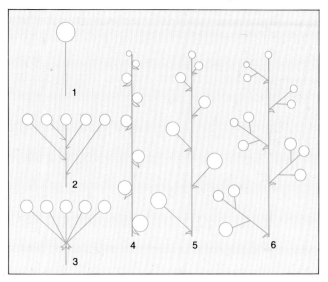

are arranged more or less spirally; however, as an alternative to the raceme of single flowers, an inflorescence may take the form of a spike, a panicle, a fascicle, an umbel or a cyme.

Inflorescences are made up of a highly variable number of flowers, perhaps just a few, as in various species of *Paphiopedilum* and *Cattleya*, or hundreds, as in *Epidendrum diffusum*. The flowers may open simultaneously or in slow succession.

**Flowers** It is of course for their extraordinary flowers that orchids are cultivated in the first place. Large or small, showy or insignificant, perfumed or unscented, long-lasting or fleeting ... they are a constant source of astonishment and delight.

These flowers normally display bilateral symmetry but in certain genera, such as *Ludisia, Mormodes*, etc., this is not evident because of the rotation of the column or the lip, which makes them appear completely asymmetrical, as if for some reason they had opened in an abnormal fashion.

The flower is attached to the stem by a stalk and at the point of insertion there is always a bract. The stalk extends to the ovary, formed of three carpellary leaves. A characteristic feature of orchids, particularly of the epiphytes, is that the ovary is not fully developed at the moment of flowering; indeed, this process is completed only if the flower is fertilized. The ovary is always inferior, i.e. situated beneath the flower parts, which are made up of three sepals, three petals and a column.

Although in the majority of orchids the sepals and petals do not

*Morphology of the flowers: 1, lip; 1a, hypochile; 1b, mesochile; 1c, epichile; 2, petal; 3, sepal; 4, column; 5, ovary; 6, flowering stem. A, Stanhopea; B, Cattleya; C, Paphiopedilum. Opposite page: above* Epidendrum cinnabarinum *(Epidendroideae); below,* Schomburgkia tibicinus *(Epidendroideae).*

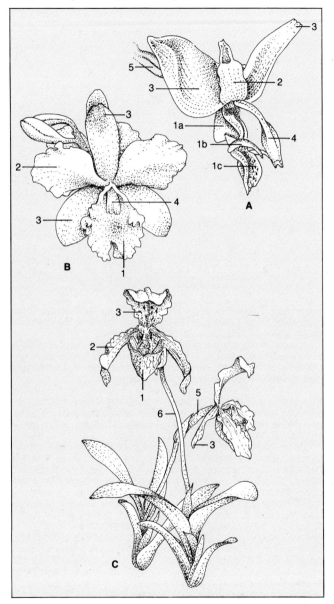

differ greatly in color and shape, the sepals, which are outside the petals, are often slightly smaller and sometimes less brightly colored. A special feature of these flowers is that one of the three petals differs morphologically from the other two: this one is called the lip (labellum). In certain genera the lip is unusually large and brilliantly colored, as in the tropical *Cattleya* orchids and the European *Ophrys* species; remarkably, in the Cypripedioideae it is pouch-shaped and in the *Coryanthes* species formed like a bucket.

In other genera, such as *Stanhopea*, the lip is so elaborate and complex that it is divided into three parts: the basal portion, known as the hypochile, is widened to form a small bowl; the middle section, or mesochile, is narrower and furnished with two stiff, twisted appendages; and the apical part, or epichile, which broadens into the shape of a triangle. In many Pleurothallidinae the lip and the petals are extremely small and virtually inconspicuous.

The lip is normally situated above the other flower parts, as, for example, in *Polystachya* and the female flower of *Catasetum*; but in many instances, because the flower is twisted through 180°, it comes to be placed underneath. In many genera there is a tubular formation of varying length at the base of the lip; this is called the spur and it usually contains nectar to attract pollinators.

Inside the sepals and petals, in continuation of the ovary, lies the column. This organ is formed from the fusion – loose or tight according to the orchid group – of the style terminating in the stigma (female sexual organ), and the stamens, generally one, terminating in the anther (male sexual organ). The reciprocal position and shape of these structures vary considerably – more between genera than between species.

Most orchid flowers are hermaphrodite. Only a few species of the genera *Catasetum, Cycnoches* and *Mormodes* have flowers of separate sexes borne by different inflorescences on the same plant, however, these are mostly produced at different times, so that self-fertilization is virtually ruled out.

In the majority of orchids the grains of pollen are collected in small masses, variable in number and size, called pollinia, located inside the anther.

**Fruits** Fertilization occurs when pollen from one flower is transported and deposited on the stigma of another flower by various animals, including many species of Hymenoptera (wasps, bees, ants), Diptera (flies), Lepidoptera (butterflies and moths), and certain birds belonging to the families Nectariniidae (sunbirds) and Trochilidae (hummingbirds).

The animal visitor, attracted by the scent and sometimes the color and shape of the flower, removes the masses of pollen that are attached by a slender filament (caudicle) to a small, sticky patch (viscidium or retinaculum) when the latter adheres to the insect's body. Subsequently, when the pollinia transported by the pollinating insect brush against the sticky stigma of another flower, they are detached from the retinaculum and adhere to the stigma.

The presence of pollen on the stigma induces the flower to fade rapidly and the ovary begins to enlarge. After some time (the period

may vary, according to species, from a few months to almost a year) the ovules are fertilized; the ovary completes its development, and the ripe fruit opens along the sutures of the three carpellary leaves, releasing the tiny seeds. These range in number from several thousand, as in many species of European orchids, to about 3,700,000 in the case of *Cycnoches chlorochilon*.

The seeds, which have no stocks of nutritive substances, are dispersed by the wind; in order to germinate they have to be invaded by symbiotic fungi (mycorrhiza) that provide the necessary substances, especially in the early stages of development.

## CLASSIFICATION AND NOMENCLATURE

The division and grouping of animals and plants on the basis of their differences and similarities has always been a subject of debate and controversy.

In recent years such discussions have been pursued with renewed energy because in addition to morphological, microscopical and macroscopical characteristics, specialists have begun to use new parameters which it has only been possible to take into consideration as a result of the latest scientific developments: for example, the chromosome number and genetic characteristics.

Although such discussions often prove sterile and perplexing, there is no denying, by and large, that taxonomy provides an opportunity for everyone involved in scientific disciplines to speak the same language.

Oncidium papilio *(Vandoideae).*

Without venturing into a discussion of the problems associated with the classification of the Orchidaceae, it is important to note that it was Lindley between 1830 and 1840 who published the first subdivision of the family into seven tribes.

Subsequently many other scholars have tackled the subject, increasing or decreasing the number of tribes and subtribes, shifting genera from one category to another, also species to different genera. Even today a universally agreed solution is still remote.

For readers unversed in the complexities of the subject, here is the recommended standardized ending according to the ICBN (International Code of Botanical Nomenclature):

| CATEGORY | ENDING | EXAMPLE |
|----------|--------|---------|
| Family | − aceae | Orchidaceae |
| Subfamily | − oideae | Vandoideae |
| Tribe | − eae | Cymbidieae |
| Subtribe | − inae | Oncidiinae |
| Genus | − | *Oncidium* |
| Species | − | *papilio* |

Every entity, animal or vegetable, is identified according to the system of binomial nomenclature devised by Linnaeus. This binomial consists of two Latin words, the first of which, describing the genus, always begins with a capital letter, and the second, indicating the species, with a small letter.

In some cases there are further subdivisions below the genus and species: subspecies, variety and form.

When two different species are crossed, the result thus obtained is called the primary hybrid and is named by hybridizers with a grex epithet consisting of one to three words which may be in any language. Individual plants of these hybrids, and more complex hybrids generated by hybrids themselves, more or less like each other, are described as clones and may be identified by one or two words, in any language, starting with a capital letter and enclosed in single quotation marks. For example:

*Oncidium forbesii* Hooker × *Oncidium marshallianum* Rchb. f.

*Oncidium* Pectorale 'Everglade'

The following classification is according to Dressler (1981):

| | |
|----------|-----------------|
| Subfamily | Apostasioideae |
| Subfamily | Cypripedioideae |
| Subfamily | Spiranthoideae |

*Below:* Oncidium forbesii.
*Opposite above:* Oncidium marshallianum; *below:* Oncidium *Pectorale 'Everglade.'*

| | |
|---|---|
| Tribe | Erythrodeae |
| Tribe | Cranichideae |
| Subfamily | Orchidoideae |
| Tribe | Neottieae |
| Tribe | Diurideae |
| Tribe | Orchideae |
| Tribe | Diseae |
| Subfamily | Epidendroideae |
| Tribe | Vanilleae |
| Tribe | Gastrodieae |
| Tribe | Epipogieae |
| Tribe | Arethuseae |
| Tribe | Coelogyneae |
| Tribe | Malaxideae |
| Tribe | Cryptarrheneae |
| Tribe | Calypsoeae |
| Tribe | Epidendreae |
| Subfamily | Vandoideae |
| Tribe | Polystachyeae |
| Tribe | Vandeae |
| Tribe | Maxillarieae |
| Tribe | Cymbidieae |

The name of the author who first described the species is shown, either in full or in abbreviated form, immediately after the specific

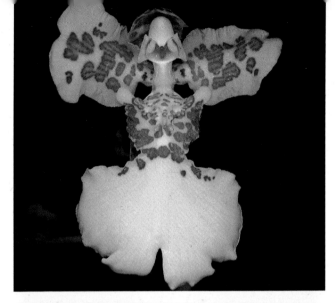

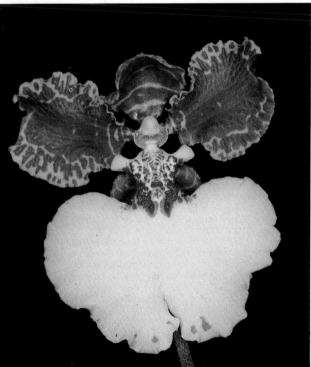

epithet. When such an author may have described the species and attributed it to another genus or another category than that given it by a later author, the name of the first author is given in parentheses and the name of the second author is then added. For example *Oncidium cebolleta* (Jacq.) Sw. indicates that the plant in question (entry 103) was originally described by N.J. Jacquin in the genus *Dendrobium*, but that it was later transferred to the genus *Oncidium* by O. Swartz.


## CULTIVATION

The cultivation of orchids nowadays poses few problems, particularly if one has at least a small greenhouse where, with up-to-date mechanical equipment and expertise, the plants can be suitably acclimatized. Those overheated stove-warmed houses of early Victorian times, where in an atmosphere redolent of a Turkish bath orchids from all over the world were killed off in their thousands, are fortunately gone for ever.

Collectors of not much more than a century ago understood little or nothing about the conditions that are necessary for orchids to thrive. Today, however, thanks to innumerable specialist books and practical guides, there is a wealth of reliable information available to anyone embarking on the cultivation of these plants.

Success in growing orchids depends on giving proper consideration to the following key factors: temperature, light, humidity, ventilation, watering and feeding.

**Temperature** Although orchids require a temperature range consistent with their places of origin, they can almost all be accommodated in one of three basic greenhouse types: the hothouse, the intermediate or temperate house, and the cool house.

In the hothouse, typically used for the *Phalaenopsis* species, the nighttime temperature should not fall below 65°F (18°C). During the day, especially in summer, it can be allowed to rise to 86-90°F (30-32°C) without the plants coming to harm.

It should be understood, of course, that any reference here to hot and cold seasons, summer and winter, applies only to temperate countries of either hemisphere, not to the intertropical regions where the majority of orchids originate and where climatic contrasts are more typically marked by a dry season and a rainy season.

In the intermediate or temperate greenhouse, suitable for the *Cattleya* orchids, the nighttime temperature should not fall below 59°F (15°C), and the daytime temperature must remain around 86°F (30°C).

The nocturnal temperature of the cool house, ideal for the *Odontoglossum* species, should not drop below 54°F (12°C). Because the plants raised here mostly come from tropical high mountain areas, the temperature by day is equally important and during summer should not be allowed to exceed 75-77°F (24-25°C).

On cold winter days, when the sun is not shining or gives insufficient heat to raise the indoor temperature, it is advisable, in all three

*Various types of support: 1, hanging basket (lower part);
2, plastic pot; 3, suspended blocks of wood; 4, cork raft.*

types of greenhouse, to set the heating system, so as to create a contrast of at least 9°F (5°C) between the night and day temperature.

Heating may be provided either through pipes (with or without radiators) or with air heaters; if the area to be heated is limited, as, say, on a patio or veranda, it may be sufficient to use a small stove that burns kerosene or some other fuel, in which case it is advisable to place the stove outside the glass in order to prevent the fumes from harming the plants.

When building a greenhouse from scratch, it is probably best to situate the longest side facing east or southeast, for north is as a rule too cold and south too hot; but much depends on the country and the method of construction.

Specialist magazines and books or, better still, friendly advice from someone who already owns a greenhouse, is helpful for avoiding elementary mistakes.

**Light**  This is of prime importance for the health of the plants and consequently their capacity to produce flowers. The unit of illumination for the measurement of light is the "foot-candle" and the instrument for this purpose is the foot-candle meter.

In this context orchids may be divided into three major groups: those that live in full shade, in full sun and in an intermediate situation. Considering that the majority of tropical orchids are epiphytic, it is the third condition that is the most common.

Although there are books and magazines that provide information on the necessary light levels for successfully raising various group of orchids, many growers, especially newcomers, may find that such absolutes can result in dangerous errors. Actually, the amount of light needed is closely linked with other factors, and only perfect familiarity with the surroundings plus experience will determine the exact amount of light necessary for cultivating particular plants. In all of the three principal subdivisions, the amount of light can be varied at different times of the year, depending on the climate of the greenhouse; generally speaking more shade should be provided in summer in order to maintain temperature and humidity within prescribed limits, and the reverse in winter. A properly balanced cultivation method will result in luxuriant plants with plump stems or pseudobulbs, well-developed leaves and regular production of flowers.

Shade in the greenhouse may be provided with nets of varying sizes of mesh and preferably of a dark color, with matting, or with white paint on the outside of the panes – all easily removable when no longer necessary.

**Humidity**  A high level of surrounding humidity is essential for plants that originally come from tropical zones; in no instance should this go below 50%.

A rise in temperature means a drop in humidity, so during the warm months of the year various methods have to be used to control levels.

In sufficiently large greenhouses the best way is to use a cooling system: a series of panels made of porous material such as paper, wood shavings, etc., over which a closed circuit supply of water can be sprayed, is fitted to one end of the greenhouse and an exhaust fan at the other end; in this way a current of cool, moist air circulates through the greenhouse, creating the desired conditions. The system can be controlled by a humidistat. Where there is less space the necessary amount of humidity can be provided by frequently spraying the paths and the areas beneath the shelves, or by using receptacles filled with water. Here the flooring should be of clay, sand or gravel, which gives off moisture. Open windows on the shady side can also help to provide suitable conditions.

**Ventilation** Air that is constantly moving is a good guarantee of health in orchids. A greenhouse for orchids, whether hot, temperate or cool, should be a pleasant environment, and the atmosphere should never be allowed to become disagreeably stale.

Useful in a modest-sized greenhouse or under glass on a veranda is a small fan and in larger greenhouses a sophisticated ventilation system is an indispensable piece of equipment.

Ventilation lowers the temperature, and dries out and eliminates any standing water that is especially likely to harm the plants when the temperature goes down. In well-ventilated surroundings plants are not seriously harmed by temperatures several degrees lower than the minimum recommended. Without proper ventilation, the lower temperature that always accompanies a rise in the humidity level encourages the development of *Botrytis cinerea*, a fungus that forms small black spots on the flowers and kills them. An adequate circulation of air, together with suitable heating of the greenhouse will actually, prevent many fungal and bacterial attacks.

**Watering** The question that experts seem to be asked most frequently is: "How should I water my orchids?"

There is no easy answer to this because it depends on many factors. Are the plants in a pot or on a raft? What soil is being used? What are the pots made of? What species are the orchids? Are they adults or young plants? Where have they been grown?

First of all, one has to know the cultural requirements of the plants, particularly in relation to their rest period. Among botanical species this period, when it exists, may be long or short, coinciding as it does with the duration of the dry season in the various countries of origin.

As a rule, plants grown on a raft, whatever the constituent material, should be sprayed very frequently, even several times a day in the growing season, and watered plentifully at least every other day. For plants kept in pots, it has to be remembered that growing media such as osmunda fiber (roots of the fern *Osmunda regalis*), tree-fern fiber (various species of *Dicksonia*), and sphagnum retain moisture longer than bark (various species of conifer), charcoal and perlite. These materials may be used either pure or mixed (usually both types together) in different proportions, according to the needs of the various plants.

Plastic pots, lighter, unbreakable and easy to disinfect, retain moisture better and longer than clay pots or baskets; furthermore it is more difficult for the roots to adhere tightly to them. Young plants, with a less-developed root system and more delicate growth, need watering more often than adults of the same species.

Given all these considerations, it is fair to say that adult plants, grown in plastic pots, with bark, should be watered on average once every 5-6 days, although this may vary by a few days either way depending on the alternative factors mentioned above.

It is best to water the orchids in the morning, preferably on a fine day, so that any standing water, harmful to the health of the plants, can disappear by evening.

Although the majority of orchids prefer water that is low in calcium, experience suggests that, apart from special cases, city water is normally suitable, especially if allowed to stand for a day or so in the tank. Rain water, if it can be collected in sufficient quantities, is ideal where there is no industrial pollution.

**Feeding** With the exception of particular cases that are listed in the notes on cultivation in each species entry, it is best to stick to precise and standardized rules when applying fertilizers made up to suitable formulas. The growing medium most commonly used today is bark, with the addition of more or less inert materials better capable of retaining moisture (peat, sphagnum, foam rubber) or of making it lighter (polystyrene, cork, pebbles), but none of these provides the plant with any food.

A fertilizer equally balanced in nitrogen, phosphorus and potassium (18–18–18), dissolved in water in the ratio of 1 gram to 1 liter (1 oz to 7½ gal), and applied once a week for approximately ten months (from late spring to early winter), and a food containing more nitrogen (30–10–10) during the remaining part of the year, which in most plants generally coincides with the resumption of new growth, will provide a sufficient supply of nutrients to give luxuriant, free-flowering plants.

There are, nevertheless, many opinions on this question. Some growers use 30–10–10 fertilizer throughout the year; some go for fertilizers with a higher phosphorus or potassium content; some give no food at all while the plants are in flower; others feed only once a month; and so on ... and all swear that their method is the only right one. A good rule to follow is to make a choice and then stick to it. Constant changes cause dangerous imbalances that seldom give satisfactory results.

Plants grown in osmunda fiber and sphagnum can be fed about once a fortnight because these materials are not entirely devoid of nutrients.

It is advisable to water the plants abundantly prior to feeding in order to wash any residues of mineral salts and to wet the roots in preparation for a new feeding. An accumulation of salts can cause serious scorching of the roots, especially if the soil is not sufficiently moist.

**Containers** The most widely collected orchids are for the most part epiphytes and can be cultivated on supports with the roots left to grow in the air. However, in practice, most orchids are grown

in pots and only a few in hanging baskets, on tree-fern rafts, on cork, or on pieces of wood. The method of cultivation is dictated by precise individual needs, and the reader is referred to the individual entries of this book for more detailed, specific guidance.

Plastic pots can be used over and over again but it is a good idea, if they are not new, to leave them soaking for a few hours in an aqueous solution of 3% commercial formalin or 7–8% chlorine bleach so as to disinfect them properly.

It is essential to provide a generous drainage layer consisting of pieces of polystyrene or loam, which should be thrown away whenever the plants are repotted.

Baskets and branches should be hardwood as this is less, likely to rot and will last longer.

Any plants grown on wood or cork, or on rafts, start off best with some tufts of sphagnum arranged around the roots, unless otherwise indicated, to provide more moisture. Plants cultivated like this are difficult to remove from their support but it is a good idea to replace the sphagnum once a year.

**Repotting** Unless there are good reasons not to do so, as may be indicated in the individual entries, orchids should as a rule be repotted every three years. The best time to do this is when the plants resume their growth and the new roots begin to sprout. In the northern hemisphere this is generally spring-summer.

Since orchid roots are fleshy and sometimes fragile, they need to be fairly dry when handled so that they heal quickly, start to grow again and branch out. Compost for repotting should therefore be moist but not waterlogged. If bark is used, choose pieces in the dimensions specifically recommended. They can be bought in three sizes: small, medium and large.

After a plant has been removed from the old compost, rotten roots, pseudobulbs and dead stems should be eliminated; the plant should then be replaced in a new pot of suitable dimensions, and positioned either center or off-center according to its structure, so that as much space as possible is left for its growth. The compost should be placed between the roots and firmly pressed down so as to give the plant stability. If necessary the plant can be tied to a stake.

It is best to use a pair of sharp scissors for removing excess growth. Sterilize them in a flame every time a new plant is handled.

Unlike most plants, orchids need not be watered after repotting for at least two weeks, until the roots start growing again. Frequent spraying and a high level of surrounding humidity will help the plants weather this critical period.

## INDOOR CULTIVATION

An inside windowsill, the corner of a well-lighted room or even a cellar will give anyone who lacks greenhouse space in the garden or on the patio the opportunity of growing orchids.

In such surroundings, however, the plants require extra vigilance and care. Because the humidity level indoors is not high enough for orchids, the pots must be placed on a layer of gravel or loam in wide, shallow, water-filled containers. It is vital that the water level should not reach the bottom of the pots since roots constantly submerged in water quickly rot. In summer frequent spraying helps to keep the humidity at the right level.

Under these conditions it is a good idea to group a number of plants together because they help one another to create the proper microclimate.

The general criteria for cultivation are the same as those recommended for greenhouse orchids but more attention has to be paid to watering because, in these conditions, the growing medium dries out rather more rapidly and only careful observation can determine when water needs to be given.

It is often suggested that the best part of the house in which to grow orchids is the bathroom, however, this room may prove quite unsuitable without the use of special equipment. The problem here is that the windows of most bathrooms are not generally big enough and do not necessarily face the right direction. Moreover, contrary to popular belief, the humidity level in the bathroom is not necessarily any higher than any other room in the house.

In rooms that have little or no natural light, orchids can still be grown successfully with the aid of artificial light. There are plenty of guides and scientific publications dealing with artificial illumination in agriculture and floriculture and in this book there is only space for a few basic guidelines, The most important point to remember is

*Above:* Bletilla striata *grown outdoors.*
*Below: how to position the plants in the home to make sure they
have the right degree of humidity.*

that above all else orchid plants need constant observation and care, and that loving attention can often achieve miracles.

There are various types of bulb that give off light of different wavelengths, from blue to infrared, indispensable for the diverse functions of the plants. Experience shows that GRO-LUX/Ws 40 watt fluorescent tubes are the best.

A series of four tubes, placed approximately 6 in (15 cm) apart under a white or metal reflector provides enough light for a group of plants positioned below them, at a distance of about 8 in (20 cm). In this instance a very important factor is the photoperiod. As a rule, illumination for 15–16 hours a day is sufficient for the majority of orchids, both species and hybrids.

However, specialized surroundings such as these are not suitable for plants like *Vanda* and similar genera that need a considerable amount of light and for others that may not flower if subjected to a constant photoperiod throughout the year. The same applies to plants such as the cymbidiums which, apart from needing plenty of light, particularly in the summer, occupy a great deal of space.

Another problem is that environments with artificial light, because of the way the equipment is arranged, maintain a fairly constant temperature, particularly from night to day, and this does not suit many orchids that need to be stimulated by diurnal differences in order to bloom.

Given these difficulties, which vary according to individual surroundings, it is worth trying to resolve specific problems in order to augment the number of species that can be grown with success.

The best results under artificial light can be obtained by growing hybrids of *Cattleya, Laelia, Brassavola*, with either small or large flowers, hybrids of *Phalaenopsis* and *Doritis*, of *Miltonia* and *Miltoniopsis*, and of *Oncidium*. There are also many botanical species that adapt to such conditions, whether grown in a pot or on a raft.

Cultivation under artificial light is inadvisable for those *Dendrobium* species that have stick-like pseudobulbs, but is highly recommended for those of compact habit or small dimensions. The same is true of the *Epidendrum* species. Excellent results can be achieved with *Encyclia, Brassia,* medium-sized *Angraecum* and all species belonging to the above-mentioned genera whose hybrids prove most satisfactory under these conditions.

One piece of advice worth bearing in mind is that everyone, even the most expert grower, loses plants; the important thing is not to be discouraged, not to give up, but to try to discover the mistake, thus ensuring success in the end.


## PESTS AND DISEASES

Orchids, like other plants, are subject to attack by various kinds of pest. A clean, airy environment with the right humidity level, suitably bright and warm, is certainly conducive to the well-being of the plants but not an absolute guarantee of it.

Even under the best conditions pests may attack the plants and only constant and attentive watchfulness can control and eradicate them.

Elimination of dry bracts and leaves and of flower stems that are no longer in bloom and will not produce flowers in years to come prevents tiny scale insects from using them as hiding places where they can multiply undisturbed.

Various species of scale insect belonging to genera such as *Coccus, Pseudococcus, Planococcus, Saissetia,* and *Diaspis* attack orchids; some are more frequently found on a single group, others parasitize a number of groups. Fortunately these insects are sensitive to readily available insecticides such as white mineral oils and malathion.

It is worth noting that because insecticides are curative and not preventive products, they should be used only when the pests are in evidence. Furthermore, these substances, although low in toxicity, are dangerous to humans. Protective masks and gloves should be worn when they are applied by spraying.

The use of products that are poisonous and potentially lethal even to humans is strongly discouraged.

To increase the effectiveness of any insecticide a surface-wetting agent should be added to the solution. The reproductive cycle of many of these tiny pests, especially in summer, is very rapid and a generation may be produced approximately once a fortnight; so in order to make sure of getting rid of them it is advisable to spray two or three times at intervals of about two weeks.

Take great care not to get any spray on flowers or buds, because this can kill them. If the plants are in flower, especially for growers who only manage to produce a few, the pests are best eliminated with a wad of cotton soaked in the required substance or with ordinary methylated spirits.

Other small parasites that harm orchids are mites (Acari). Both red spider and false spider mites attack and damage the upper and lower surfaces of the leaves of many orchid genera, and this can be serious if these are not quickly counteracted. The leaf surfaces of the plants attacked by these mites take on a typically cloudy, silver-gray appearance in the initial phase, or the damage may show up as tiny withered pits on other plants. Once the pest is identified, it is essential to take action quickly with acaricides.

Although ants are not orchid pests as such, they may create problems by feeding on the sugary secretions of scale insects and aphids and thus help to spread them. Ants can be kept under control with specific spray preparations.

It is a good idea to sprinkle granules or metaldehyde periodically over floors and benches to discourage slugs and snails, which in a single night can damage or destroy an inflorescence, a young leaf or newly forming roots.

It is beyond the scope of this book to describe the various bacteria and fungi (molds) that are likely to attack the roots and aerial parts of orchids; suffice it to say that these organisms are by far the most dangerous for the plants, and can kill them very quickly if not immediately controlled.

Shriveled, almost dehydrated leaves are symptoms of root rot. The plant must at once be removed from the pot, and the parts affected, which look black and soggy, cut off with sterilized scissors.

Similarly, brown patches of soft tissue, which quickly grow bigger, on leaves and pseudobulbs are signs of fungal or bacterial disease.

Some orchid genera are more susceptible to attack by certain species of fungi or bacteria than others, but all these parasites are capable of causing extremely serious damage.

Standing water, surroundings that are not sufficiently heated or ventilated, excessive humidity, soil that retains too much moisture, are all conditions that help to spread these agents of disease. Regular spraying, every two to three months, with fungicides is indispensable for preventing such problems. There are many effective products on the market, either copper or sulfur-based, or synthetic; some are more suitable for spraying on the leaves, others for watering around the roots.

It is unwise to mix the various products either with each other or with insecticides, unless they are known for certain to be compatible.

Fungicide for watering the roots can be added, in doses of 1 gram to 1 liter (1 oz to 7½ gal), to the water in which fertilizer has been dissolved. The wounds made by the removal of parts damaged by rot should be sprinkled with fungicidal powder.

Sooty mold is a mold that covers the aerial parts of orchids, though not penetrating them, like a thin black veil, thriving on the sugary secretions produced by the plants themselves. It can be removed with cotton dipped in methylated spirits or in fungicide.

*Botrytis cinerea*, under conditions of low temperature and high humidity, especially at night, produces small brown spots, which may turn violet in time, on the flowers. If conditions remain favorable, it will spread rapidly. The remedy is to get rid of all infected flowers and correct the climatic conditions.

Viral diseases can also be a nightmare for beginners. Any tiny spot on the leaves, any alteration in the color of the flowers tends to be diagnosed as a virus attack. But although it is quite true that viral diseases are virtually incurable, it is some consolation to know that many plants can survive a virus infection for years, regularly producing flowers.

It is not always easy, without equipment for tests and analyses, to diagnose a viral attack correctly, because the same virus may provoke different symptoms in the same plant or the same symptom on plants of different species; furthermore, some bacteria cause manifestations on leaves that are similar to those of certain viruses.

In cases that are particularly evident, however, such as marked change of color in flowers and leaves, and the formation of unpigmented patches, usually arranged in strips, it is best to throw away both the plant and the pot, and to sterilize under a flame the scissors that may have come into contact with the plant. In doubtful cases, which are more common, after getting rid of those parts of the plant that show suspicious changes, it is a good idea, if you do not want to throw the plant out, to put it in a place apart from the others, bearing in mind that the virus needs a transporting agent to pass from one plant to another and that care is required to avoid contagion — not always as easy as might be imagined.

## HYBRIDIZATION AND MULTIPLICATION

The majority of flowering orchid plants on the market nowadays are hybrids of *Cymbidium, Paphiopedilum, Phalaenopsis,* or *Cattleya,* and their cost need not deter anyone from buying them. Yet not much more than a century ago hybridization and the consequent sowing of orchids were practically unthinkable.

The first flowering hybrid was a cross between *Calanthe furcata* and *Calanthe masuca* in 1856, performed by Dominy, head gardener of the orchid section of the firm J. Veitch and Sons of Exeter, in England. It was named by John Lindley, *Calanthe* Dominyi. Other crosses followed, all carried out in those early years by Dominy, and in due course other growers emulated his work.

In 1863 the first intergeneric hybrid was created: *Cattleya mossiae* × *Laelia crispa*: and in 1892 the first trigeneric hybrid appeared: *Sophronitis grandiflora* × *Laeliocattleya* Schilleriana.

Today there are more than 70,000 hybrids and every year several thousand more are registered. These are raised not only by established firms but also by amateurs.

The science of genetics has made enormous progress and although we now know a great deal about genetic incompatibility and the hereditary features of flowers intended for use as mother and father plants much still remains to be discovered. Experimentation consequently still plays an important role in hybridization and attempts are frequently made to cross botanical species that have rarely or never previously been used in experiments both with each other and with complex hybrids, to cross complex hybrids with one another, and to intercross species of different genera. The purpose of all this activity is to discover new forms, colors and patterns that approach as far as possible the ultimate ideals of beauty for each of the various types of orchid flower concerned.

Even after Dominy had learnt how to cross two different orchid plants (thus creating the first hybrid) with the intention of obtaining a seed capsule, only the very first part of the problem of hybridization had been solved.

For many years myriads of minute seeds obtained from the fruit were sprinkled around the base of the mother plant, since this was the only method deemed possible to produce new plantlets.

The breakthrough came in 1885 when the German botanist Frank discovered a relationship between the seeds of wild orchids and fungus hyphae, showing how important the latter were for the development of the seeds.

In the first decade of the present century Bernard and Burgeff separately published several papers on their research into the isolation and cultivation of various species of symbiotic fungi, demonstrating their importance in the development of orchid seeds.

In 1922 in place of the fungus hyphae that provided the tiny seeds with nutritive elements Knudsen substituted an artifical medium in which starch was replaced by simple sugars, with the addition of various mineral salts. The first growing medium prepared by Knudsen was later improved and adapted to the needs of different orchid groups, both by Knudsen himself and other botanists.

*Capsule of a* Cattleya *hybrid six months after fertilization.*

The era of growing orchids on an industrial scale was thus initiated. Such modern systems now enable 90% of seeds to germinate.

In this context it is worth mentioning that although there may be an apparent incompatibility between two plants selected as parents of a potential hybrid – e.g. two complex hybrids of *Phalaenopsis* – often their actual incompatibility is only revealed later, with the death of the flower a few days after receiving pollen, or several weeks later with the drying up of the ovary which has started to swell, or with the ripening of the capsule and the formation of sterile seeds without embryos.

Until the beginning of the 1960s when Morel applied to orchids the system of meristemic multiplication which was subsequently used for other agricultural plants, individual orchids were multiplied only by division of a plant into two or more sections. The distribution of especially beautiful and desirable clones was thus a rather slow process and such plants were often genuine rarities.

Explanted meristemic cells – i.e. small groups of as yet undifferentiated cells at the apex of a newly forming shoot – are capable, in particular artificial growing conditions, of producing protocorms which, after subsequent treatment, develop into new plantlets identical to the mother plant. This method was first used to free especially interesting clones of viruses, because these cells are immune to such viruses; but in due course its principal purpose was to produce, within a very short time, a large number of plants that had the same characteristics as the parent, notably the same splendid flowers.

Successful explantation of apical meristemic cells is not yet possible in all genera of orchids: paphiopedilums, for example, do not respond to the practice and multiplication of the most highly prized clones is still done by division.

Meristemic reproduction has certainly helped to popularize the growing of orchids and to bring down considerably the market prices of even the loveliest clones. On the other hand, because of its guaranteed success, it poses something of a threat to the practice of hybridization which may sometimes be uncertain and often disappointing but which stimulates research into obtaining new forms.

In 1906 Sander began to publish a list of hybrids that has been produced, with the names of the parents and hybridizers; today this register is continued by the Royal Horticultural Society, London, and is known as "Sander's List."

Every year, all over the world, many specialist orchid shows are organized, with a jury of at least three members examining the plants submitted for judging, and awarding prizes based on various criteria. The names of particularly beautiful clones are given the initials of awards received and the names of the societies awarding them. The most common are listed below:

FCC (First Class Certificate), 90 or more points out of 100, equivalent to a GM (Gold Medal); AM (Award of Merit), 80–89 points, equivalent to a SM (Silver Medal); HCC (Highly Commended Certificate), 75–79 points, equivalent to a BM (Bronze Medal).

*Below:* Odontonia *Vesta 'Charm.'*
*Opposite above:* Brassocattleya *Languedoc 'Patrick'*;
*Opposit below:* Odontioda *Picasso 'Rubis'.*

*Hand-painted copper engraving of an orchid,*
*taken from the* Dictionnaire Universel d'Histoire Naturelle *published*
*between 1841 and 1849 under the direction of Charles d'Orbigny*

AOS = American Orchid Society; AOC = Australian Orchid Council; HOSI = Hawaiian Orchid Society Inc.; JOS = Japan Orchid Society; RHS = Royal Horticultural Society; SIO = Societá Italiana Orchidee (Italian Orchid Society); TOS = Taiwan Orchid Society, etc.

Every three years a World Conference on Orchids is held in a different country. In 1987 it was in Japan (Tokyo); in 1990 it will be in Auckland, New Zealand.

## 1 ACACALLIS CYANEA Lindl.
(Maxillarieae, Zygopetalinae)

**Synonyms** *Aganisia coerulea* Rchb. f., *A. tricolor* Batem.
**Origin** Brazil, Colombia, Venezuela.
**Description** Medium-sized plant with visible rhizome. The pseudobulbs are fusiform, compressed, and slightly rugose, often covered with dry bracts; they are generally equipped with a single elliptic leaf, glossy on the upper side, and normally measuring a little over 8 in (20 cm) long and at least 2½ in (6 cm) wide. The curved inflorescence sprouts from the base of the mature pseudobulb and has a variable number of flowers that open in succession. The flowers, 1½–2 in (4–5 cm) in diameter, never open fully; they are periwinkle blue, almost white near the base of the petals and sepals and have a bronze or reddish-purple lip. They appear in summer.
**Cultivation** The plant is usually grown on rafts of tree fern or on cork, but can also be kept in a basket or pot, preferably one that is broad and shallow, in which case the compost must be enriched with sphagnum. *A. cyanea* needs humidity, both in surroundings and growing medium, and does not like being repotted or divided; such operations should therefore be carried out only when absolutely necessary.

---

## 2 ACINETA SUPERBA (HBK) Rchb. f.
(Cymbidieae, Stanhopeinae)

**Synonyms** *Anguloa superba* HBK, *Peristeria humboldtii* Lindl.
**Origin** Colombia, Ecuador, Panama (?), Venezuela.
**Description** Large plant. The ovoid pseudobulbs, up to about 4 in (10 cm) long, bear 2–3 lanceolate, plicate leaves, 16–20 in (40–50 cm) long and 3 in (7–8 cm) wide. The pendulous inflorescences 8–12 in (20–30 cm) long, have very big flowers, the color of which varies from creamy white to beige, heavily marked with darkish orange-red spots. The flowers, waxy and long-lasting, never open completely. They appear in spring.
**Cultivation** This species must be grown in a fairly broad mesh basket to allow the inflorescences to protrude in all directions. Sphagnum or osmunda fiber is recommended as a growing medium. During growth the species requires frequent watering; later it is advisable to give it a period of rest at a lower temperature to enable the pseudobulbs to mature, and to stimulate flowering.

## 3 AERANGIS LUTEO-ALBA (Kraenzl.) Schltr. var. rhodosticta (Kraenzl). J. Stewart
(Vandeae, Aerangidinae)

**Synonyms** *Angraecum mirabile* Hort., *A. rhodostictum* Krzl.
**Origin** East Africa.
**Description** This is perhaps the loveliest of the 50 or so species of the entire genus. Medium-small plant, monopodial in structure, with a very short, prostrate stem. The leaves are alternate, linear, slightly coriaceous, 4–5 in (10–12 cm) long, with an unequally bilobed apex. The axillary, curved, pendulous inflorescence, sometimes more than 8 in (20 cm) long, bears numerous flat flowers in two rows, 1½ in (3–4 cm), ivory white with an orange-scarlet column, which open simultaneously. There is a spur of 1½ in (3–4 cm) at the base of the lip. The orchid flowers in winter and spring.
**Cultivation** This species, together with others of the same genus, prefers to grow on cork, on a block of wood or on a raft to which its roots can adhere and enjoy good air circulation: stagnant water is, in fact, particularly harmful. During the summer, which is also the period of growth, the species needs daily spraying, while in winter it is enough to water it once every 5–6 days. If well cultivated, the stems of this species may branch forming small groups which, while in flower, will make a fine spectacle with their numerous spikes.

---

## 4 AERIDES ROSEA Loddiges ex Lindl. & Paxt.
(Vandeae, Sarcanthinae)

**Synonyms** *Aerides williamsii* Warn., *A. fieldingii* Williams.
**Origin** Sikkim to Assam, Laos, Vietnam, Thailand and Burma.
**Description** Plant with monopodial structure, slow-growing, up to 8–10 in (20–25 cm) high. The leaves are opposite, bilobed, slightly carinate, about 8 in (20 cm) long, the basal leaves often drooping. The inflorescence, sometimes over 16 in (40 cm) long, is axillary, pendulous, with large numbers of closely packed flowers, 1 in (2–3 cm) in length, that open in succession; color deep pink flushed with white at base of petals and sepals. The orchid flowers in spring.
**Cultivation** This species, like all the rest belonging to the genus, prefers to grow in baskets filled with coarse material such as bark and pieces of charcoal, so that the long roots can, after taking a grip, protrude from the container. The plants do not like to be disturbed and should therefore be left in the same container for years. Watering should be regular throughout the year, slightly more frequent in summer.
**Hybrids** *Aerides* is commonly hybridized with *Vanda, Phalaenopsis, Arachnis* and *Renanthera*.

## 5 ANCISTROCHILUS ROTHSCHILDIANUS

O'Brien

(Arethuseae, Bletiinae)

**Origin** Tropical Africa.

**Description** Medium-small plant. The characteristic pseudobulbs are conical and rather easily cracked, about ½ in (1 cm) tall, with 2 leaves at the apex; these are lanceolate or elliptic, flexible, 4–8 in (10–20 cm) long, deciduous. The pubescent flower stem sprouts from the base of the pseudobulb, sometimes more than one, and bears 2–5 flowers. These are white or pink, with a lip of deeper color, fairly large and showy considering the size of the plant, opening in succession and long-lasting. The orchid flowers in winter.

**Cultivation** Neither this species nor *A. thomsonianus* (Rchb. f.) Rolfe, the only members of the genus, are very common in collections. They are best grown in small pots with a light, well-drained medium, preferably with an addition of sphagnum. Watering should be frequent during plant growth so as to keep compost moist at all times; later this should be reduced to allow the growing medium to dry out between applications. Repot only when the plant is throwing out too many shoots.

---

## 6 ANGRAECUM DISTICHUM Lindl.

(Vandeae, Angraecinae)

**Synonym** *Mystacidium distichum* (Lindl.) Pfitz.

**Origin** Tropical Africa.

**Description** Small plant that seldom grows to a height of more than 4–6 in (10–15 cm). The leaves, compressed, triangular, imbricate, coriaceous, glossy, persistent for many years, completely enfold the stem, which branches out freely, forming small tufts. The tiny single white flowers appear in large numbers from the leaf axils. The species may flower at various times of the year, often more than once.

**Cultivation** The plant is easy to grow. Because of the long, thin roots, it is best grown in small pots with compost that is finely broken up, light and well drained. Regular watering throughout the year and good illumination are indispensable. Repotting can be done in spring, if considered necessary, and does not normally cause the plant any problems.

## 7 ANGRAECUM SESQUIPEDALE Thou.
(Vandeae, Angraecinae)

**Synonym** *Aeranthus sesquipedale* (Thou.) Lindl.
**Origin** Madagascar.
**Description** Large plant which, with age, may exceed 3 ft (1 m) in height. The leaves, opposite, linear, very coriaceous, slightly pruinose, with a bilobed apex, are at least 10 in (25 cm) long and 1 in (3 cm) wide; the aging basal leaves fall, uncovering the stem. The roots are very thick and rather stiff, sprouting, from the aerial part of the stem. The axillary inflorescences, generally shorter than the leaves, have 5–6 very big stellate flowers, creamy white, waxy, with a spur that may measure more than 12 in (30 cm) long; the perfume is especially heavy at night, and in its native land the species is pollinated by moths. The orchid flowers in winter.
**Cultivation** The plant is easy to grow. Because of its potential dimensions, it is suitable for raising in a pot, and it adapts to any kind of growing medium provided this is well drained. Watering should be regular throughout the year. Repot only when strictly necessary; at that time, care must be taken not to damage the roots, particularly the more fragile ones growing out of the compost. The stems branch readily so that very large plants can be obtained.
**Hybrids** The species is hybridized with others of the same genus: *A.* Veitchii (= *A. eburneum* × *A. sesquipedale*).

---

## 8 ANGULOA CLOWESII Lindl.
(Maxillarieae, Lycastinae)

**Origin** Colombia, Venezuela.
**Description** Large plant that, if well grown, will form a good specimen. The pseudobulbs, pyriform, compressed and channeled, are at least 4–5 in (10–12 cm) long, with a number of obovate, plicate, deciduous leaves, 24–28 in (60–70 cm) long. The flowering stems, sheathed in bracts, 10–12 in (25–30 cm) long, sprout in number from the base of the pseudobulbs each bearing a single large, waxy flower; the color varies from creamy white to deep yellow, and the typical cup shape causes these plants to be known as "tulip orchids." The orchid flowers in spring.
**Cultivation** *A. clowesii* is a terrestrial species that is nevertheless best grown in a pot with a well-drained medium; if bark is used it is advisable to add sphagnum or osmunda fiber. During the period of growth the medium must be kept wet and the surroundings moist and airy. For successful flowering, give the plant, after full development, a period of rest at a lower temperature for several weeks.
**Hybrids** *Anguloa* is hybridized with *Lycaste* (= *Angulocaste*).

## 9 ANSELLIA AFRICANA Lindl.
(Cymbidieae, Cyrtopodiinae)

**Synonyms** *A. africana* var. *nilotica* Bak., *A. gigantea* Rchb. f.
**Origin** Central and southern Africa.
**Description** Fusiform pseudobulbs, up to 28 in (70 cm) tall, which sprout from a very short rhizome that is difficult to see when the plant is well grown. Leaves lanceolate, about 8 in (20 cm) long, sheathing the pseudobulb, persistent in groups of 6–8 only toward the apex; old pseudobulbs are often without leaves. Terminal or subterminal inflorescence, about 8 in (20 cm) long, branched, with very long-lasting flowers of about 2 in (5 cm). This species is commonly called the leopard orchid because the flowers, which vary widely in size, range from ivory white to deep lemon yellow, sometimes with fairly dark brownish spots. The lip is bright yellow, trilobed, and characterized by 2–3 longitudinal crests. The orchid flowers from winter to early spring.
**Cultivation** The plant should be grown in a pot proportionate to its size. It needs damp, well-drained compost during the growing period, but this should be allowed to become drier to enable the pseudobulbs to mature after their complete development.

---

## 10 ARACHNIS Blume
(Vandeae, Sarcanthinae)

**Origin** Philippines, Solomon Islands, New Guinea, Southeast Asia.
**Description** Generally large plant with monopodial structure. The stem of certain species may easily measure 10–13 ft (3–4 m). The leaves are linear or ligulate, coriaceous, stiff, alternate and well spaced. The axillary inflorescences are stiff, fairly long, branched or simple, and made up of a variable number of waxy, long-lasting flowers that open in succession. The flowering period varies according to species, but in temperate regions flowers usually appear in summer and autumn.
**Cultivation** The *Arachnis* orchids are generally easy to grow but seldom flower outside their countries of origin because they need a consistently hot and very humid climate, with a great deal of light.
**Hybrids** Certain species of *Arachnis* are interbred to obtain flowers for cutting and for sale, being improvements on the original species. *A.* Maggie Oei (*A. flos-aeris* × *A. hookeriana*) is one of the commonest of the commercial hybrids.

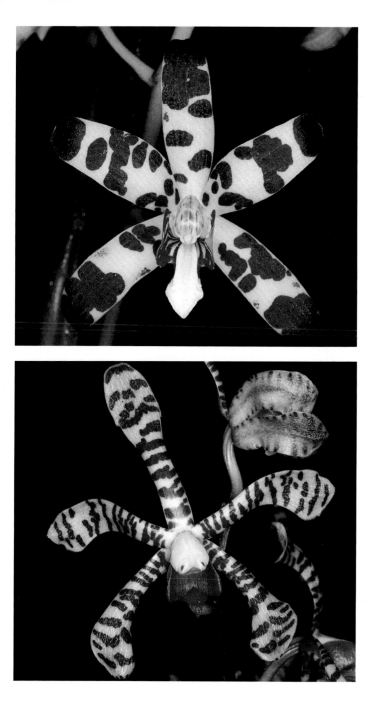

## 11 ASCOCENTRUM Schltr.
(Vandeae, Sarcanthinae)

**Description** Medium or medium-small plants with monopodial structure. The leaves are linear, stiff, alternate and carinate, measuring not more than 10–12 in (25–30 cm) in length; they may have two teeth at the apex and they cover the base of the stem. The axillary inflorescences, sometimes more than one at a time, are erect, more or less as long as the leaves; they comprise many flowers of ½–1 in (1–3 cm), very close together and opening in succession. The flat flowers, conspicuous and long-lasting, are brightly colored, yellow, orange-red, scarlet or purple with a spur. They appear in spring-summer.

**Cultivation** The three or four species belonging to this genus are easy to grow. It is generally advisable to raise them in baskets in a compost prepared from a mixture of bark, charcoal and crock, etc. The roots grow abundantly, confined at first to the container and then breaking free; consequently it is best to place the plant in a bigger basket without disposing of the first one. The plants enjoy a humid atmosphere and need frequent watering, particularly in summer. They should also be positioned in good light.

**Hybrids** In the last few decades growers have taken advantage of affinities to hybridize the genera *Vanda* and *Ascocentrum* (*Ascocenda*), mainly to reduce dimensions, which in the case of the *Vanda* species, often get out of hand, and also to increase flowering capacity and color range. *Ascocentrum* is also crossed with *Neofinetia* (= *Ascofinetia*) and with *Phalaenopsis* (= *Asconopsis*).

Above left: *Ascocentrum miniatum* (Lindl.) Schltr.
Origin: Java, Northeast India, Indochinese peninsula.

Above right: *Ascocentrum curvifolium* (Lindl.) Schtr.
Origin: Northeast India, Indochinese peninsula.

Below left: *Ascocenda* Yip Sum Wah.

Below right: *Ascocenda* Suk Sumran Beauty.

## 12 ASPASIA EPIDENDROIDES Lindl.
(Cymbidieae, Oncidiinae)

**Synonym** *Aspasia fragrans* Kl.
**Origin** Costa Rica, Guatemala, Honduras, Nicaragua, Panama, northern part of South America.
**Description** Medium-sized plant with ovoidal, compressed pseudobulbs, fairly high on the rhizome, about 4 in (10 cm) long and covered around the base by two or three distichous, bracteal leaves. The two apical leaves are lanceolate, rather coriaceous though flexible, 6–12 in (15–30 cm) long. The erect basal inflorescences, about 8 in (20 cm) long, bear a few long-lasting, spotted flowers that open in succession in summer.
**Cultivation** The six or so species, all easy to grow and free-flowering, can be raised in a pot, in a basket with any soil, or on a raft. Plentiful watering during growth should be followed by a rest period of about a month after flowering.
**Hybrids** *Aspasia* is hybridized with several other genera of Oncidiinae; certain clones of *Brapasia* (*Aspasia* × *Brassia*) are particularly attractive.

## 13 BARKERIA SPECTABILIS Batem. ex Lindl.
(Epidendreae, Laeliinae)

**Synonym** *Epidendrum spectabile* (Batem. ex Lindl.) Rchb. f.
**Origin** El Salvador, Guatemala, Mexico.
**Description** Medium-small plant with cylindrical pseudobulbs 2–6 in (5–15 cm) tall and with a diameter of about ¼ in (0.5 cm), covered by dry bracts. The alternate, oblong-lanceolate, flexible leaves are deciduous. The apical inflorescence bears a variable number of spotted, lilac flowers, about 1 in (3 cm) long, not very long-lasting but showy. They open successively. The plant flowers in winter.
**Cultivation** The species belonging to this genus usually grow best on a raft of tree fern or cork. During plant growth it is advisable to water regularly, then to allow a rest period at a lower temperature and with plenty of light, at which time the plant loses some or all of its leaves.

## 14 BIFRENARIA TETRAGONA (Lindl.) Schltr.
(Maxillarieae, Bifrenariinae)

**Synonym** *Maxillaria tetragona* Lindl.
**Origin** Brazil.
**Description** Medium-sized plant. The pseudobulbs, close together on the rhizome, are pyramidal with 4 well-marked points 3–3½ in (8–9 cm) tall, rugose, yellow-green, with a single coriaceous, petiolate leaf, at least 12 in (30 cm) long, at the apex. The very short basal inflorescences are formed of 4–5 waxy, campanulate flowers that are greenish yellow with a deep purple lip. They last some days and give out a highly aromatic, not always pleasant, scent. The flowers appear in summer.
**Cultivation** The *Bifrenaria* species grow well in baskets or shallow pots. The growing medium may consist of bark, osmunda or tree-fern fiber, and should be kept moist but not waterlogged. When new growth is complete, slightly reduce watering. The plant must be well grown to ensure good flowering. Repot only when the growing medium is decomposed or if the container is too small.
**Hybrids** *Bifrenaria* has been hybridized with *Lycaste* ( = *Lyfrenaria*) but plants are rarely available commercially.

---

## 15 BLETILLA STRIATA (Thunb.) Rchb. f.
(Arethusae, Bletiinae)

**Synonym** *Limodorum striatum* Thunb.
**Origin** China, Japan.
**Description** Medium-large terrestrial species. The pseudobulbs are subterranean, rounded and compressed. The erect stem bears several oblong-lanceolate, plicate, flexible leaves, up to 16 in (40 cm) long and about 2 in (5 cm) wide, green sometimes flecked with white. The lax terminal inflorescence, about 8 in (20 cm) long, consists of several lilac flowers of about 1½ in (3–4 cm) that open in succession from late spring well into summer.
**Cultivation** *B. striata* can also be grown in the open in a sheltered place as an ordinary garden plant; but although it adapts to any growing medium, results are obtained in light, leafy soil, well manured in spring. It does well in a sunny position shaded from midday heat. In winter it loses its leaves; the small bulbs can be left in the ground. The species can also be grown successfully in a pot.

## 16 BOLUSIELLA TALBOTII (Rendle) Summerh.
(Vandeae, Aerangidinae)

**Origin** Tropical Africa.

**Description** Small plant of monopodial structure with a very short stem. The leaves, arranged fanwise, are transversely compressed, imbricate, slightly succulent and 1¼–2½ in (3–6 cm) long. The axillary, simple inflorescence, shorter than the leaves, is made up of very tiny campanulate flowers that open simultaneously and last about one week. The flowers appear in winter.

**Cultivation** The ten or so species of the genus *Bolusiella* are difficult to grow and are therefore found only in specialized collections. These plants do best if grown on small blocks of wood or on cork, with a little sphagnum to keep the very slender roots moist. At the hottest time of year, or when atmospheric humidity tends to decrease, spray the small plants frequently to prevent them shriveling.

---

## 17 BRASSAVOLA NODOSA (L.) Lindl.
(Epidendreae, Laeliinae)

**Synonyms** *Brassavola venosa* Lindl., *Epidendrum nodosum* L.

**Origin** From Mexico to Panama, Venezuela.

**Description** The short, cylindrical pseudobulb has a single linear, fleshy, stiff leaf, channeled on the upper surface, 10–12 in (25–30 cm) long. The pendulous inflorescence has a variable number of flowers about 3 in (7–8 cm) in diameter, long-lasting and ranging from pale green to white, the white lip spotted with purple at the base. The orchid flowers at various times of the year, generally winter to spring.

**Cultivation** Because of its habit this species is best grown in a basket or on a raft. Water plentifully during growth, then reduce moisture gradually but do not stop; make sure, especially, that raft specimens do not shrivel. The plant branches readily.

**Hybrids** This genus is widely used for crossing with many other genera: *Cattleya, Laelia, Sophronitis, Epidendrum, Diacrium*, etc.

## 18 BRASSIA VERRUCOSA Lindl.
(Cymbidieae, Oncidiinae)

**Synonyms** *Brassia aristata* Lindl., *B. brachiata* Lindl., *Oncidium verrucosum* (Lindl.) Rchb. f.

**Origin** Guatemala, Honduras, Mexico, Venezuela.

**Description** Medium-large plant with ovoid, compressed pseudobulbs, 2½–4 in (6–10 cm) tall, situated close together on the rhizome. The two apical leaves, elongated, elliptic, coriaceous but flexible, are 8–16 in (20–40 cm) long. The one or two basal inflorescences are over 20 in (50 cm) long and are made up of a variable number of cream or pale green flowers with very long, slender sepals and petals; they open in rapid succession. The orchid flowers in spring.

**Cultivation** The species that belong to this genus are generally easy to grow and are best raised in a pot or basket with a light, not too coarse, medium. Watering should be regular throughout the year. Repotting and division present no special problems. *B. verrucosa* grows easily.

**Hybrids** *Brassia* is widely used to hybridize other genera belonging to the Oncidiinae.

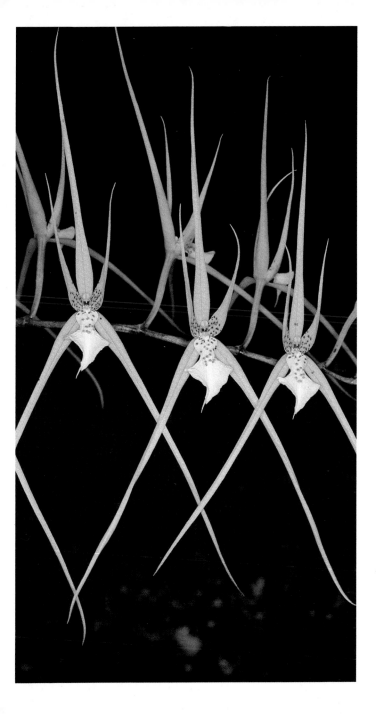

## 19 BROUGHTONIA SANGUINEA (Sw.) R. Br.
(Epidendreae, Laeliinae)

**Synonyms** *Epidendrum sanguineum* Sw., *Broughtonia coccinea* Lindl.

**Origin** Cuba, Jamaica.

**Description** Medium-small gray-green plant. The globose pseudobulbs are strongly compressed, about 2 in (4–5 cm) tall, growing close together, often prostrate. The apical leaves, generally two, are oblong, erect, stiff, 4–8 in (10–20 cm) long. The flower stem is apical, slender, stiff, at least 8 in (20 cm) long; the terminal part bears at least 5–6 flowers about 1 in (2–3 cm) in diameter, which open in succession. These are pink, red or purple and last a few days. The plant flowers once a year but at different periods.

**Cultivation** The species grows best on cork, on a block of wood or on a raft of tree fern. While making growth it needs frequent watering; then water is gradually reduced until development is complete.

**Hybrids** *B. sanguinea* has been crossed with various genera and species belonging to the same subtribe, the aim being to reduce the dimensions of the plants and to obtain new shapes and flower colors. Particular success has been experienced in crossing various species and hybrids of *Cattleya* (= *Cattleytonia*). Such hybrids are best grown in small or medium-size pots.

Above: *Broughtonia sanguinea* (Sw.) R. Br.
Below: *Cattleytonia* Keith Roth 'Roma' (*C. bicolor* × *B. sanguinea*).

## 20 BULBOPHYLLUM FALCATUM (Lindl.) Rchb. f.
(Epidendreae, Bulbophyllinae)

**Synonym** *Megaclinium falcatum* Lindl.
**Origin** Tropical Africa.
**Description** Medium-small plant with visible rhizome. The pseudobulbs are normally ovoid-elongate, about 2 in (5–6 cm) long, with 3–4 fairly pronounced points. The two oblanceolate or lanceolate, coriaceous, stiff apical leaves, are about 4 in (10 cm) long and ½–¾ in (1–2 cm) wide. The basal inflorescence consists of a rachis about 8 in (20 cm) long, with a flattened terminal portion. The small flowers are dark red and orange, numerous but short-lived, and appear on either side of the rachis, opening successively. The orchid flowers from winter to spring.
**Cultivation** This plant, like the majority of other *Bulbophyllum* species, can be grown on a block of wood or in a basket; in the latter case the growing medium should be a blend of bark, sphagnum and osmunda fiber. Abundant watering during the growth period should be slackened off later but not stopped. Repot only when the compost shows signs of decomposition.

---

## 21 BULBOPHYLLUM LEPIDUM (Bl.) J.J.Sm.
(Epidendreae, Bulbophyllinae)

**Synonym** *Cirrhopetalum gamosepalum* Griff.
**Origin** Tropical Africa.
**Description** Medium-small plant with visible rhizome. The ovoid pseudobulbs are ½–¾ in (1–2 cm) tall and bear at the apex a lanceolate, coriaceous leaf, about 4 in (10 cm) long and about ¾ in (2 cm) wide. The flower stem, basal, about 8 in (20 cm) long, bears 7–10 yellowish, red-spotted flowers, about 1 in (2–3 cm), typically arranged in an umbel and with long, fused, lateral sepals: these are two of the characteristics that lead some botanists to ascribe this and similar species to the genus *Cirrhopetalum*. The flowers of *B. lepidum* give out a disagreeable smell of rotting organic matter which stimulates certain species of fly to pollinate them. This characteristic is very common among other species of the same genus. The orchid usually flowers from summer to winter.
**Cultivation** This species is also best grown in a basket or on a block of wood, in warm, moist, buoyant surroundings. Watering should be regular throughout the year.

## 22  BULBOPHYLLUM LOBBII Lindl.
(Epidendreae, Bulbophyllinae)

**Origin** Borneo, Indonesia, Indochinese peninsula.

**Description** Medium-sized plant. The ovoid pseudobulbs, placed well apart on the rhizome, are 1–2 in (3–5 cm) long and bear at the apex a single oblong, coriaceous, erect, petiolate leaf, 4–10 in (10–25 cm) long and up to 3 in (7 cm) wide. The erect flower stem, 4–6 in (10–15 cm) long, sprouts from each node of the rhizome. The single waxy flower is fairly deep yellow, variably streaked with brown, long-lasting and 2½–4 in (6–10 cm) in size. The plant normally flowers in summer.

**Cultivation** This species of *Bulbophyllum*, although one of those most prized by collectors for its particularly large and attractive flowers, is not easy to grow and does not always flower as abundantly as many other species of the genus. It is advisable to grow it in a basket or in a low but fairly broad pot, in a well-drained compost. Good results are also obtained with plants grown on a raft of tree fern or cork, or even on a block of wood. Although watering should be regular throughout the year, care should be taken not to overwater, especially when new plant growth is forming, for this is likely to rot if water is left standing. Repotting should be done only when the compost starts to break up.

**Hybrids** Various species of *Bulbophyllum* have been crossed with one another but the resultant hybrids are not always easy to find.

## 23  CALANTHE TRIPLICATA (Willem.) Ames
(Arethuseae, Bletiinae)

**Synonym** *Calanthe veratrifolia* (Willd.) R. Br.
**Origin** From southern India through Southeast Asia to Australia and Fiji.
**Description** Large terrestrial species of the *Calanthe* group with persistent leaves and extremely small pseudobulbs. The leaves are elliptic-lanceolate, fairly long, petiolate, with a pubescent underside, 16–24 in (40–60 cm) long and 4–6 in (10–15 cm) wide. The erect flower stem, longer than the leaves, is pubescent and the upper third bears many clustered white flowers, about 2 in (5 cm) long, which open in succession and are long-lasting. The orchid flowers in spring and summer.
**Cultivation** It is best to grow this species in a well-drained pot with compost that is always kept moist. Repot every year after flowering.
**Hybrids** Various species of *Calanthe* are crossed with one another with excellent results. Highly interesting clones can also be obtained with *Phaius* ( = *Phaiocalanthe*) and *Gastorchis* ( = *Gastocalanthe*).

## 24  CATASETUM BARBATUM (Lindl.) Lindl.
(Cymbidieae, Catasetinae)

**Synonyms** *Catasetum proboscideum* Lindl., *C. spinosum* Lindl.
**Origin** Brazil, Guyana, Peru.
**Description** Medium-sized plant. The pseudobulbs are fusiform, close together, about 6 in (15 cm) tall. The leaves are membranous, oblanceolate or lanceolate, distichous, sheathing the pseudobulb, deciduous, 8–14 in (20–35 cm) long and 2–3 in (5–8 cm) wide. The inflorescence, basal, normally comprises greenish flowers of one sex only: the male inflorescence is curved, stiff, usually not longer than the leaves, with many fringed flowers; the female is erect, shorter than the male, with fewer, rather hooded flowers. A feature of all male flowers of *Catasetum* is the spring mechanism that projects pollen for quite a distance as soon as it is touched. The orchid flowers from winter to spring.
**Cultivation** The *Catasetum* species are, as a rule, easy to grow, preferably in small pots, with any kind of well-drained medium. Watering, abundant during the period of growth, should be stopped after flowering and leaf drop until new growth commences.

Left: male inflorescence.
Right: female inflorescence.

## 25 CATASETUM FIMBRIATUM (C. Morr.) Lindl.
(Cymbidieae, Catasetinae)

**Origin** Tropical regions of South America.

**Description** Medium-small plant. The fusiform pseudobulbs are about 6 in (15 cm) long. The leaves are membranous, oblanceolate or lanceolate, opposite, deciduous, about 8–16 in (20–40 cm) long and 2–3 in (5–8 cm) wide. The inflorescence is often longer than the leaves, stiff, curved, fairly lax, made up of many flowers, more numerous in the males. The green and pinkish flowers, with a waxy lip and dentate margins, measure about 2 in (4–5 cm), open in succession and last several days. The orchid flowers in spring and summer.

**Cultivation** The *Catasetum* species are best grown in pots that are suspended to allow the long, curved inflorescences to grow without hindrance. Well-grown plants may yield two inflorescences to each pseudobulb produced during the year. It is best to grow *Catasetum* in a temperate or intermediate greenhouse, however, if treated carefully excellent results can also be obtained in the hothouse.

## 26 CATASETUM PILEATUM Rchb. f.
(Cymbidieae, Catasetinae)

**Synonym** *Catasetum bungerothii* N. E. Br.

**Origin** Brazil, Trinidad, Venezuela.

**Description** Medium-large plant. The fusiform pseudobulbs are at least 8 in (20 cm) long and sheathed by the base of the leaves. The leaves are lanceolate, membranous, opposite, deciduous, 10–18 in (25–45 cm) long and 3–5 in (7–12 cm) wide. The male inflorescence, at least 12 in (30 cm) long, comprises large white flowers, variously flushed with yellow or green, opening successively and short-lasting. The orchid flowers in winter.

**Cultivation** The *Catasetum* species, although able to withstand temperatures a few degrees higher than recommended, are best grown in a warm, moist, well-ventilated place; in fact, high temperatures and low humidity may encourage red spider infestations. Repotting is advisable every year after flowering and leaf drop.

## 27 CATTLEYA Lindl.
(Epidendreae, Laeliinae)

**Origin** Tropical Central and South America.

**Description** Classification of this genus still gives rise to much controversy; the 60 or so species ascribed to it differ considerably and are divided into two groups – single-leaved and two-leaved. The single-leaved forms are generally plants with medium-length pseudobulbs, somewhat swollen and set well apart. They bear a single apical, fairly erect, coriaceous leaf, variable in form according to species. The inflorescence rarely consists of more than 4 large, often brilliantly colored flowers, which open simultaneously and last 2–3 weeks. Each single flower may measure more than 8 in (20 cm) across, as in *C. warscewiczii*, and is often highly scented. Exceptions in this group are *C. araguaiensis* and *C. luteola*, both of which seldom grow to more than 6 in (15 cm) in height, with flowers of about 2½ in (6 cm) in diameter. The two-leaved species generally have fairly slim pseudobulbs, varying in length from a few centimeters, as in *C. aclandiae*, to almost 3 ft (1 m), as in *C. amethystoglossa* and *C. leopoldii* which have 2 or sometimes 3 coriaceous, variously shaped leaves at the apex. The flowers are as a rule smaller that those of the other group, usually not over 4 in (10 cm) long. *C. aurantiaca* produces the smallest flowers of the entire genus, barely about 1½ in (3–4 cm) in length. In various species the inflorescence consists of numerous flowers, there may be as many as 20 in *C. bowringiana*.

**Cultivation** The species belonging to the genus *Cattleya* are mostly epiphytic plants from a variety of environments within a very large distribution area, consequently they have different cultivation requirements that must be met if an abundance of flowers is desired. However, the enormous advances in hybridization have resulted in the development of thousands of clones, obtained by innumerable crosses, with similar and far simpler cultivation requirements; furthermore, these clones produce a greater abundance of flowers that are lovelier, richer in color and longer-lasting. The great advantage of hybridization is that the rest period required by many botanical species has been dispensed with. Thus watering and feeding can be kept up regularly throughout the year. Cattleyas, though they are intermediate greenhouse plants, can withstand a temperature of 86–90°F (30–32°C) without any trouble, provided the atmospheric humidity is over 60 percent. It is a good idea for this humidity content to fluctuate between 50 percent and saturation over 24 hours. It is also advisable to keep the surroundings properly and constantly ventilated; this will prevent water from collecting on the surface of the growing medium and on the leaves, since an excess of standing water can damage the flowers. A cattleya that is cultivated under ideal conditions with the right balance of light, humidity, temperature, watering and feeding, will produce plump pseudobulbs, upright leaves of a consistent, light green color, and magnificent flowers from every new shoot. Indications that these factors in cultivation are not properly balanced are given by weak pseudobulbs incapable of supporting foliage, leaves that are too dark green or yellowish, and absence of flowers. Cattleyas should be regularly repotted and divided every three years;

*Cattleya bowringiana* O'Brien.

this does no harm to the plants if done when the new roots and new shoots are beginning to appear after flowering. Plants that flower in the autumn or winter therefore need to be repotted and divided in early spring; those that flower in spring need attention in early summer; and those that flower in summer need attention either very early in spring or immediately after flowering, not too late in the season because in autumn vegetative activity slows down and the new root system will not be sufficiently developed by winter. To be sure of producing flowers, each division should comprise at least three or four pseudobulbs with one or more new developing shoots. It is also advisable to use some form of support, such as a bamboo stake, and attach the pseudobulbs by binding raffia around the portion between the leaf and the pseudobulb itself. The best growing medium to use is bark, although cattleyas can also be grown in osmunda fiber and some small or medium-sized botanical species on tree-fern rafts.

Below: *Cattleya warscewiczii* var. *gigas* Rchb. f.
Opposite above: *Cattleya araguaiensis* Pabst.
Opposite below: *Cattleya aurantiaca* Batem. ex Lindl.) P.N. Don.

**Hybrids** The genus *Cattleya* is commonly crossed with the following genera: *Laelia, Brassavola, Sophronitis, Epidendrum, Schomburgkia, Broughtonia*, etc. Hybrids have been obtained with five different genera, and the results are often as extraordinary as their names: *Rothara* (*Cattleya* × *Brassavola* × *Epidendrum* × *Schomburgkia* × *Sophronitis*), and *Fergusonara* (*Cattleya* × *Brassavola* × *Laelia* × *Schomburgkia* × *Sophronitis*). For some years many breeders have also attempted to produce plants of smaller size, with flowers that are also smaller but just as beautiful as those of the originals. In this way they have obtained *Cattleya* hybrids which, when adult and in flower, stand in a pot scarcely bigger than a coffee cup. To this end the genus *Cattleya* has been crossed mainly with *Broughtonia, Sophronitis, Diacrium* and certain species of *Laelia*.

Below: Lc. Butterfly Bell 'Queen of Formosa'.
Opposite above: Blc. Malworth 'Orchidglade' FCC/AOS.
Opposite below: Blc. Autumn Glow 'Green Goddess' HCC/CST.

## 28 CIRRHAEA DEPENDENS (Lodd.) Rchb. f.
(Cymbidieae, Stanhopeinae)

**Synonyms** *Cirrhaea fuscolutea* Lindl., *Cymbidium dependens* Lodd., *Gongora viridipurpurea* H.K.
**Origin** Brazil.
**Description** Medium-sized plant with narrowly grooved pseudobulbs, about 1½ in (4 cm) tall, bearing one apical, petiolate, lanceolate leaf, 10–12 in (25–30 cm) long and about 2½ in (6 cm) wide. The basal inflorescence is at least 10 in (25 cm) long, pendulous and dense and consists of numerous long-lasting, waxy flowers, about 1½ in (4 cm) long, which vary in color from ocher to brown, and open simultaneously. The orchid flowers in spring and summer.
**Cultivation** Because of the long inflorescences, it is best to grow this plant in a basket, although it can also be grown in a pot, if suspended. The light, well-drained compost should be enriched with sphagnum or osmunda fiber. A short rest period is necessary after flowering. Repot and divide only when essential.

---

## 29 COCHLEANTHES DISCOLOR (Lindl.) R.E.
(Maxillarieae, Zygopetalinae)

**Synonyms** *Chondrorhyncha discolor* (Lindl.) P.H. Allen, *Warrea discolor* Lindl.
**Origin** Costa Rica, Cuba, Honduras, Panama, Venezuela.
**Description** Medium-small plant. Lacking pseudobulbs, the stem is very short and often branches at the base to form small tufts. The flexible pale green leaves are oblanceolate, pointed, about 8 in (20 cm) long and tightly imbricate. The erect, basal inflorescences, shorter than the leaves, have a single, long-lasting flower with curved sepals and petals, creamy white flushed with green. The petal tips are tinged with violet and the lip is violet with a white border. The flowers appear from spring to autumn.
**Cultivation** All species of the genus require special care in growing. They can be raised either in a pot or in a basket provided the growing medium is moist and well drained and preferably enriched with sphagnum or osmunda fiber. Stagnant water is particularly harmful to these plants, which are subject to rotting generated by fungi or bacteria. Repotting and division should be carried out only when essential.

## 30 COCHLIODA NOEZLIANA (Mast.) Rolfe
(Cymbidieae, Oncidiinae)

**Synonym** *Odontoglossum noezlianum Mast.*
**Origin** Peruvian Andes.
**Description** Medium-small plant with ovoid, slightly compressed, dark green pseudobulbs, about 2 in (4–5 cm) tall. The one or two apical leaves are linear, thin, 4–6 in (10–15 cm) long; the other leaves are shorter, deciduous, enfolding the base of the pseudobulb. The inflorescence is basal, curved, sometimes branched, about 8 in (20 cm) long, with numerous orange-red flowers of long duration which open in succession. The orchid flowers in spring and early summer.
**Cultivation** *C. noezliana*, like other species of the genus, is not an easy plant to grow because it needs a rather low temperature, not exceeding 75–77°F (21–25°C) in summer, plenty of humidity, good ventilation and illumination, and a well-drained compost. The plant is subject to attack by pathogens if overwatered. Feeding should be given in half doses, ideally in alternate weeks.
**Hybrids** *C. noezliana* is widely used for crossing with *Odontoglossum, Oncidium, Miltonia* etc., mainly to confer its typical coloration on the progeny.

## 31 COELIA BELLA (Lemaire) Rchb. f
(Arethuseae, Bletiinae)

**Synonym** *Bothriochilus bellus Lemaire.*
**Origin** Guatemala, Honduras, Mexico.
**Description** Medium-sized terrestrial species. The pseudobulbs are ovoid-globose, close together, about 1½ in (4 cm) tall. The leaves are linear-lanceolate, flexible, up to 24 in (60 cm) long and about ½ in (1–2 cm) wide. The inflorescence is lateral, erect, about 6 in (15 cm) long, consisting of a few long-lasting 1½–in (4–cm) flowers that are white with pink tips. These appear in spring and summer.
**Cultivation** This species must be grown in pots proportionate to the dimensions of the plants, but never too big. The growing medium should be well drained and porous in order to avoid excessive moisture, which can harm the newly developing plant growth. In winter, when the plant is virtually resting, watering should be reduced to prevent the pseudobulbs from shriveling. The species dislikes repotting and division, so these procedures should be undertaken only when absolutely necessary.

## 32 COELOGYNE CRISTATA Lindl.
(Coelogyneae, Coelogyninae)

**Synonym** *Cymbidium speciosissimum* D. Don.
**Origin** Himalayan region.
**Description** The ovoid pseudobulbs, set apart on the permanently visible rhizome, are about 2 in (4–5 cm) long and bear two narrowly lanceolate, flexible leaves 6–12 in (15–30 cm) long and about 1 in (2 cm) wide. The basal inflorescences produced by the pseudobulb of the year are 4–6 in (10–15 cm) long and have 4–5 white flowers the lip of which has five golden-yellow, fringed ridges or keels. The plants branch freely, forming large specimens. Flowering is in spring.
**Cultivation** The species can be grown either in a pot or in a basket, with any fairly soft, well-drained compost. Great care must be taken with watering at the beginning of the new growth period because standing water can cause rotting. Division and repotting should be done only when absolutely necessary.

---

## 33 COELOGYNE MASSANGEANA Rchb. f.
(Coelogyneae, Coelogyninae)

**Synonym** *Coelogyne densiflora* Ridl.
**Origin** Java, Malaysia, Sumatra, Thailand.
**Description** Medium-large plant with conical-ovoid pseudobulbs, 3–4 in (8–10 cm) tall, close together on the rhizome, bearing two apical leaves, petiolate, elliptic-obovate, coriaceous and flexible, about 8 in (20 cm) long and at least 2 in (5 cm) wide. The basal, pendulous inflorescence may measure over 16 in (40 cm) in length and bears a few dozen cream and brown flowers, each enclosed by a large bract. The flowers, very delicate and short-lasting, open simultaneously. A well-grown plant produces several inflorescences at the same time. The orchid may flower at various times of year, usually in summer, and sometimes twice.
**Cultivation** This species, like all those of the same genus originating in tropical zones, must be kept in a hothouse or in the warmest part of a temperate greenhouse. It is best grown in a basket or in a pot with soft, well-drained compost. For an abundance of flowers the plants should be encouraged to branch, so it is advisable to repot and divide them when the container becomes too small.

## 34 COELOGYNE PANDURATA Lindl.
(Coelogyneae, Coelogyninae)

**Origin** Borneo, Malaysia, Sumatra.

**Description** Medium-large plant with oblong, compressed pseudobulbs, set well apart on the rhizome, about 4 in (10 cm) long, with two petiolate, elliptic-lanceolate leaves, coriaceous and flexible, 8–18 in (20–45 cm) long and about 3 in (6–7 cm) wide. The curved inflorescence, 8–12 in (20– 30 cm) long, is composed of well-spaced flowers, about 4 in (10 cm) in diameter, pale green with a typically black-streaked lip. The orchid generally flowers in autumn.

**Cultivation** Like most of the species belonging to the genus, (there are over 150), this orchid is best grown in a basket or in a pot, preferably suspended, in a light, not too coarse, medium, because of the rather soft roots. If well grown, it branches freely and may flower more than once a year.

## 35 COMPARETTIA FALCATA Poepp. and Endl.
(Cymbidieae, Oncidiinae)

**Synonym** *Comparettia rosea* Lindl.

**Origin** Central America, Caribbean, northern regions of South America.

**Description** Medium-small plant. The very small, compressed pseudobulbs bear a single leaf, erect, coriaceous, 2–7 in (5–18 cm) long and about 1 in (3 cm) wide. The inflorescence, basal, curved, lax and usually about 12 in (30 cm) long, is composed of fairly large numbers of pink-purple 1 in (2 cm) flowers, each with a curving spur at the base of the lip. The orchid flowers in autumn and winter.

**Cultivation** The species, like others of the same genus, is usually grown on a raft of tree-fern fiber to which the abundantly produced thin roots can adhere firmly. It is essential to keep the growing medium damp at all times, never letting it dry out completely. The plant flowers readily but if not well rooted should not be allowed to bloom, otherwise it will wither and die.

**Hybrids** In the last thirty years various species of *Comparettia* have been hybridized with one another and with species of related genera such as *Oncidium, Rodriguezia* and *Odontoglossum.*

## 36 CORYANTHES SPECIOSA Hk.
(Cymbidieae, Stanhopeinae)

**Origin** Guatemala, Honduras, hot northern regions of South America.

**Description** Medium-large plant with conical, elongated pseudobulbs at least 4 in (10 cm) tall, densely channeled, with two lanceolate leaves, 12–16 in (30–40 cm) long and 3 in (7–8 cm) wide, at the apex. The basal, pendulous inflorescences, about 12 in (30 cm) long, carry 5–6 ochrous-yellow flowers of a truly extraordinary shape, which open simultaneously. The lip has the form of a bucket in which an abundance of highly scented liquid is secreted by two tubercles situated at the base of the column. The orchid flowers in summer.

**Cultivation** The *Coryanthes* species have to be grown in baskets to enable the inflorescences to snake out in all directions. It is best to use a well-drained medium that retains moisture without becoming soaked. After the completion of new growth, although a true rest period is not necessary, it is advisable to reduce watering slightly. These plants do not take to repotting or division, so these procedures should be carried out only when strictly necessary.

## 37 CYCNOCHES HAAGII B.R.
(Cymbidieae, Catasetinae)

**Synonym** *Cycnoches versicolor* Rchb. f.

**Origin** Brazil.

**Description** Medium-sized plant with cylindrical-fusiform pseudobulbs at least 10 in (25 cm) tall. The leaves are deciduous, lanceolate, broad, membranous, plicate and alternate, 4–12 in (10–30 cm) long. The axillary, curved inflorescences bear many long-lasting flowers that open simultaneously. The green and white flowers are usually unisexual and the typical form, especially of the male flowers, gives rise to the common name of swan orchid which is applied to this and other species of the genus. The orchid flowers from autumn to winter.

**Cultivation** These plants are easy to grow and need special care only when being repotted. Between applications of water the compost should be allowed to dry out completely. After flowering the leaves turn yellow and fall off; this is the time to repot, usually every year. Watering should be stopped until new roots begin to develop from the new shoots. Overwatering or watering at the wrong time may cause root rot.

## 38 CYMBIDIUM Sw.
(Cymbidieae, Cyrtopodiinae)

**Origin** China, India, Indonesia, Japan, Indochinese peninsula.

**Description** Medium and large plants with fairly well-developed pseudobulbs generally ovoid in shape, very close together, sometimes absent as in *C. dayanum* Rchb. f. The largest species, such as *C. lowianum* Rchb. f. and *C. tracyanum* Rolfe, form impressive groups. The leaves are generally straight, narrow, and pointed, 8–12 in (20–30 cm) long, coriaceous but flexible, sheathing the pseudobulbs; sometimes, as in *C. devonianum* Lindl. and Paxt., they are lanceolate, 4–8 in (10–20 cm) long, usually fairly numerous on each pseudobulb. In autumn the leaves of old pseudobulbs turn yellow and fall off, leaving only the surrounding basal sheath portion. The inflorescences, formed of many clustered flowers, are basal, fairly long, erect, curved or pendulous, and are never branched. The individual flowers, varying considerably in size and color according to species, are long-lasting, firm, and sometimes highly scented. Today, as a result of hybridization, an incredible number of clones are appearing on the market. These clones, the product of multiple crosses designed to produce bigger flowers, to extend the range of colors

Below: *Cymbidium eburneum* Lindl.
Opposite above: *Cymbidium tracyanum* Rolfe.
Opposite below: *Cymbidium suavissimum* Sander ex Curtis.

and shades, and to improve the shape and arrangement on the stem, have lost the typical form and colors as well as many of the cultivation requirements of the species, and instead the leaves and the flower itself have acquired a fairly uniform shape and size. The flowering period of the species and hybrids is variable, and may occur at any time of the year, although the hybrids particularly are less likely to flower during the two or three hottest months. In all cases the plants flower once a year.

**Cultivation** It is virtually impossible to provide generally applicable information on the cultivation of this genus since it comprises over 50 species most of which seldom appear in collections. However the species can justifiably be divided into two major groups: those from warm zones, which have to be raised in a hothouse, and those from temperate-cold zones, which must be kept in a cool or temperate greenhouse. Species with a pendulous inflorescence, such as *C. devonianum, C. finlaysonianum* Lindl., *C. madidum* Lindl., etc., are best grown in hanging baskets. Hybridization and meristematic propagation of the best clones have involved this type of orchid more than any other, so that they are now virtually mass-produced for sale both as cut flowers and flowering plants. Thus *Cymbidium* hybrids are freely available and popular because they flower abundantly, are easy to cultivate and are very hardy. The following guidance on cultivation is therefore confined to such hybrids, both with big flowers (standards) and miniatures. The adult plants are generally large and indeed may become unwieldy if repotted without being divided. They should be grown in pots appropriate to their size, bearing in mind that they will remain untouched for at least three years, and fairly deep, considering the potential root spread. Although a wide variety of synthetic mediums are used for growing *Cymbidium* orchids on an industrial scale in order to lower production costs, e.g. fiberglass, plastic and perlite, it is as a rule better to grow the plants in a standard medium of moderately thick pieces of bark for adult plants and thinner pieces for young ones. Water should be plentiful and regular during the period of new growth, so that the medium is always moist; thereafter it is gradually reduced, to allow the compost to dry out between applications. The pot must have a generous drainage layer. Although *Cymbidium* hybrids, both standard and miniature, are the result of multiple crosses of hot and cold greenhouse species, they flower much better if kept in moderately cool surroundings, well ventilated, and with a humidity level fluctuating between 50 percent to saturation. An indispensable factor for obtaining the best results is a marked temperature contrast between day and night. At the hottest time of year, when the temperature in some regions may rise to 82–86°F (28–30°C), it is essential that it go down at night to below 68°F (20°C). This cultural requirement is a limiting factor in the widespread growing of *Cymbidium* hybrids in hot tropical areas. During the hottest parts of the summer day, the plants benefit from frequent spraying with water. Of all the widely distributed orchids, the *Cymbidium* species need the most light, especially after the growth of new vegetation and before the commencement of the flowering season. Too much light during flowering alters the color of the flowers, darkening some and lightening others. Slight shade when the sun is at its peak is enough to protect the leaves from harmful scorching; at such times it is advisable to control increase of temperature by good ventilation and water spraying

Above left: *Cymbidium* Lillian Stewart 'St Sherrie' HCC/AOS.
Above right: *Cymbidium* San Francisco 'Stephenson'.
Below left: *Cymbidium* Cariga 'Canary' AM/RHS.
Below right: *Cymbidium* Jungfrau 'Dos Pueblos' AM/AOS-RHS.

rather than by giving more shade. Repotting and division of adult plants are operations that require some energy. The large clumps of pseudobulbs can be divided only with a good saw, and any that are cut in half or show the slightest wounds should be rejected. The almost inextricable mass of roots should be loosened and freed from those that are dead or broken. Old pseudobulbs without leaves should be detached from the stumps and may be repotted if they retain a portion of rhizome: after a while one of the dormant buds will almost invariably begin to develop and produce a small plant that will flower after a few years. *Cymbidium* orchids, if regularly and properly tended, are extremely luxuriant plants, and particularly resistant to pathogenic disease. However, this same resistance may also render useless periodic applications of fungicides for preventive purposes. Moreover, the plentiful production of leaves and clumping of pseudobulbs may encourage the development of parasites such as scale insects and red spider. Warm, dry surroundings also tend to favor red spider infestation. To combat this it is advisable to dose the plant repeatedly every two or three months during the nonflowering period, with insecticides or acaricides in conjunction with a surface-active agent. *Cymbidium* orchids, which are kept indoors while in flower, should later be placed in the open air in a brightly lit spot out of the direct rays of the midday sun. In countries with a temperate climate the plants can be kept outdoors from spring to autumn. In regions with very mild winters, where the temperature never falls below 32°F (0°C), they can be planted out directly in light, well-drained soil, like ordinary garden plants, and will often give excellent results.

**Hybrids** All the standard and miniature *Cymbidium* orchids cultivated today are hybrids derived from multiple crosses, not only of species but chiefly of other hybrids. The first *Cymbidium* hybrid to be produced was *C. eburneum-lowianum* in 1889, from the crossing of *C. eburneum* with *C. lowianum*. Then during the early years of the 20th century, a group of invaluable clones began to appear which helped to originate some of the most famous of modern hybrids, the first of them being *C.* Alexanderi 'Westonbirt' FCC/RHS in 1922. From the 1950s onward even better results were obtained and a large number of hybrids made lasting impressions. The great increase in *Cymbidium* growing dates from the 1960s when, for the first time, Morel applied the technique of meristematic propagation to these fascinating plants. The firm of Vacherot and Lecoufle was the first to adopt the method on a commercial scale and soon the best clones of a succession of extraordinary hybrids were available to the world market. Each year saw new hybrids added to the list of those already famous: Babylon, Balkis, Burgundian, California, Featherhill, Jungfrau, Kurun, Lilian Stewart, Miretta, Remus, Rio Rita, Samarkand, San Francisco, Sayonara, Via Real, Vieux Rose... and many more.

*Cymbidium* miniatura Silvia Miller 'Paola'

## 39  CYPRIPEDIUM CALCEOLUS L.
(Cypripedioideae)

**Synonyms** *Cypripedium luteum* Aiton, *C. flavescens* De Cand., *C. pubescens* Willd.

**Origin** Temperate zones of North America, Asia and Europe.

**Description** The yellow lady's slipper, or moccasin flower, is a medium-sized ground plant. The stem is pubescent, erect, about 8 in (20 cm) long, and sprouts from an underground rhizome. The 3–5 leaves sheathing the stem are plicate, membranous, elliptic-lanceolate, 2–8 in (5–20 cm) long and 1–4 in (3–10 cm) wide. The flowers, 1–2, or rarely 3, per stem are showy and so variable that at one time there were thought to be two different species. Sepals and petals range from yellow-green to various shades of brown; the lip is yellow. The plant blooms from April to July in wetland areas from Newfoundland to Texas and in chalky soil in Mediterranean zones.

Also native to the eastern U.S. are *C. reginae* (showy lady's slipper) growing to 3 ft (1 m) with white petals and sepals and a beautiful pink lip; *C. candidum* (white lady's slipper) with greenish-yellow flowers with a white lip; *C. arietinum* (ram's-head lady's slipper) with greenish or crimson sepals and petals and a rather curious, large, pointed pouch that is white marked with crimson lines. These three orchids have stems that bear both leaves and flowers and all bloom in spring. Another eastern native, *C. acaule* (pink lady's slipper) has a pink lip that is slit in front; the leaves and flower-stalk rise from an underground stem. Native to the western U.S. are *C. californicum*, with a dozen small flowers on the tall stems. The flowers have greenish-yellow to brown sepals, yellow petals, and a white lip. *C. montanum*, growing in the western mountains, has 1–3 fragrant flowers with purple-brown sepals and petals and a purple-veined white lip. All these natives are protected by law.

**Cultivation** These native garden plants require plenty of moisture but do well in almost any well-drained, neutral to slightly acid soil that is rich in humus. Grow them in a shady spot where they get considerable sunlight. Avoid heavy shade.

## 40    DENDROBIUM AGGREGATUM Roxb.
(Epidendreae, Dendrobiinae)

**Synonym** *Dendrobium lindleyi* Stend.
**Origin** Southern China, India, Indochinese peninsula.
**Description** Medium-small plant. The pseudobulbs are fusiform, angular, 2–3 in (5–8 cm) long, silver-gray, clustered close together. The leaves are single, oblong, coriaceous, erect, each growing from the tip of a pseudobulb, and are 3–4 in (7–10 cm) long and about 1 in (2.5–3 cm) wide. A single inflorescence, lax and pendulous, 4–8 in (10–20 cm) or more in length, is produced by each pseudobulb, growing towards its tip; it is formed of many delicate, long-stalked orange-yellow flowers of about 1 in (3 cm) which open almost simultaneously. The orchid flowers in spring.
**Cultivation** This easily cultivated plant is normally grown on cork or on a block of wood, to which it clings tightly, tending to cover it. It needs plentiful, frequent watering during growth and then, in order to flower abundantly, a one-two month dry period at a lower temperature and with more light.

**Note** Recent studies have shown that plants formerly named *D. aggregatum* should be known as *D. lindleyi* if there are many flowers on the inflorescence, and *D. jenkinsii* if there are only one or two flowers.

---

## 41    DENDROBIUM ANTENNATUM Lindl.
(Epidendreae, Dendrobiinae)

**Origin** New Guinea and adjacent islands.
**Description** Medium-large plant. The erect, stick-like pseudobulbs are about 24 in (60 cm) long. The leaves are coriaceous, narrowly oblong, persistent for many years. The lax inflorescences, stiff, horizontal or curved, are formed of a dozen or so flowers and grow toward the tip of the pseudobulb. The pale green and white flowers, 2–3 in (6–8 cm) tall, with erect, spirally twisted petals, are long-lasting and open successively. The orchid flowers in summer.
**Cultivation** *D. antennatum* is a delicate species to grow, more so than other similar species, for example *D. stratiotes*; it needs a constant temperature, high humidity, good ventilation and regular watering throughout the year, rather more frequently during the period of growth. The plant is best kept in baskets or small pots, and the growing medium should be fairly soft and very well drained. Most suitable is bark, perhaps with an addition of crumbled charcoal. The use of sphagnum and osmunda is not recommended because these materials retain too much moisture, which can be harmful to the plants.

## 42 DENDROBIUM CHRYSOTOXUM Lindl.
(Epidendreae, Dendrobiinae)

**Synonym** *Dendrobium suavissimum* Rchb. f.
**Origin** Southern China, northeastern India, Indochinese peninsula.
**Description** Medium-sized plant. The pseudobulbs are fusiform-elongate with longitudinal grooves, 6–12 in (15–30 cm) long, packed closely together at the base. The 3–5 leaves at the apex of each pseudobulb are elliptic-lanceolate, coriaceous, about 4 in (10 cm) long and 1–1½ in (3–4 cm) wide, and persist for many years. The inflorescence which sprouts from the apical nodes is curved and lax, made up of 15–20 long-lasting flowers. These are golden-yellowish but with reddish streaks on the orange-yellow disk on the lip. The orchid flowers mainly in spring.
**Cultivation** This species, like many others of the same genus, should be grown in small pots, even though these may appear out of proportion to the plant size. Watering, abundant during the growing period, should be gradually reduced in order to allow the medium to dry out between applications. Dendrobiums do not like being repotted or frequently divided, and this species is no exception; therefore, such operations should be attempted only when the plants have filled the pot. It is worth mentioning that many species flower for many years in succession, even from old pseudobulbs, so it is best to eliminate as few as possible in the course of repotting and division.

## 43 DENDROBIUM CUCUMERINUM Macleay ex Lindl.
(Epidendreae, Dendrobiinae)

**Origin** Australia.
**Description** Small plant. The slender, creeping rhizome branches freely and gives out thick roots. The leaves, fairly far apart, are ½–¾ in (1–2 cm) long and are characteristically shaped liked a small cucumber. The short inflorescence sprouts from the rhizome and is composed of a few cream or whitish flowers, about ½ in (1 cm) across, which do not last long and have an unpleasant scent. The orchid flowers in spring.
**Cultivation** The species is easy to grow either on rafts of tree fern or on cork; in the latter case sphagnum can be inserted between the root tufts. Watering should be regular throughout the year, but the substratum needs to dry out between applications, especially when the plant is fully grown.

## 44 DENDROBIUM MACROPHYLLUM A. Rich.
(Epidendreae, Dendrobiinae)

**Synonyms** *Dendrobium ferox* Hassk., *D. veitchianum* Lindl.
**Origin** Indonesia, Philippines, New Guinea.
**Description** Medium-large plant. The pseudobulbs, shaped like an elongated spindle and slightly compressed, are erect, angular, 8–12 in (20–30 cm) long, greenish-yellow streaked with brown. The leaves, generally 3 to each pseudobulb, are apical, persistent, coriaceous and elliptic. The inflorescence is apical, erect or curved, about 12 in (30 cm) long, made up of some 15 pale green flowers 2 in (4–5 cm) across, which have hairy sepals and are long-lasting. The orchid generally flowers in spring.
**Cultivation** This species is best grown in a pot or basket, with a well-drained medium in which it can grow freely. Watering should be regular throughout the year, as should temperature and humidity. It is advisable to repot and divide the plant only when the container has obviously become too small.

## 45 DENDROBIUM NOBILE Lindl.
(Epidendreae, Dendrobiinae)

**Origin** Himalayan area, southern China, Indochinese peninsula.
**Description** Medium-sized plant. The erect pseudobulbs, resembling knotty sticks, are about 16 in (40 cm) long, greenish-yellow in color. The leaves, one to each node, lasting for two years, are coriaceous, oblong, about 2–4 in (5–10 cm) long and about 1 in (2 cm) wide. The short inflorescences, composed of 2–4 flowers, are produced from the nodes of the pseudobulbs whether or not the latter bear leaves. The flowers, of long duration, are white, variously streaked with lilac and with a characteristic brown spot on the disk of the lip.
**Cultivation** *D. nobile* is certainly the most frequently cultivated species of this genus; it is not very difficult to grow, even for a beginner. It flowers abundantly provided that in autumn, when fully developed, it is given a rest period of at least 2 months in the cool part of the greenhouse and water is almost completely withheld.
**Hybrids** In the last 15 years particularly, this species has undergone multiple hybridizations, which have produced some beautiful and very floriferous clones, often richly colored; one of these, illustrated on the right is *D.* Utopia 'Messenger' AM/AOS.

Left: *Dendrobium nobile* var. *pendulum*.
Right: *Dendrobium* Utopia 'Messenger' AM/AOS.

## 46 DENDROBIUM PARISHII Rchb. f.
(Epidendreae, Dendrobiinae)

**Origin** Southern China, Indochinese peninsula.

**Description** This species, in most cases, fails to form impressive, well-grown specimens, even though the pseudobulbs, stick-like but generally drooping, about ½ in (1–2 cm) in diameter, may grow to a length of over 20 in (50 cm). The leaves, more or less elliptic, slightly coriaceous, deciduous, are 2½–3 in (6–8 cm) long and, as in most *Dendrobium* species, sheathe the internodes of the pseudobulb. The flowers, which are usually in pairs, and sprout simultaneously from the node, measure about 2 in (5–6 cm) across and last 2–3 weeks. They are amethyst-purple and have two deep red spots on each side of the throat of the lip. They appear in spring and summer.

**Cultivation** This species is easy to grow. It is best kept in pots or small hanging baskets with very well-drained compost. Watering should be frequent during the growth period but should then be stopped for several weeks. During the rest period the species sheds its leaves and requires much more light than normal in order to produce inflorescences.

## 47 DENDROBIUM SENILE Par. et Rchb. f.
(Epidendreae, Dendrobiinae)

**Origin** Indochinese peninsula.

**Description** Small-medium plant. The pseudobulbs are very hairy, resembling elongated, rather twisted spindles, seldom exceeding 3 in (8 cm) in length. The 2–3 persistent leaves, obovate or lanceolate, situated near the apex of the pseudobulb, are 2 in (4–5 cm) long. The entire plant is covered with a short, dense white down. The yellow flowers, single or paired, sprout from the apical nodes of the pseudobulb, have a waxy consistency and measure about 2 in (6 cm) in diameter. The orchid flowers in spring and summer.

**Cultivation** This species is, as a rule, best grown on cork or on a block of wood, but it can also do well in a small pot; the compost, not too coarse, can be given an addition of crumbled charcoal. It is essential for the pot to be well drained so as to avoid any standing water. After the completion of new plant growth it is advisable, though not obligatory, to allow a short rest period of about 2 weeks. Repotting should be done only when the compost begins to break up.

## 48 DENDROCHILUM GLUMACEUM Lindl.
(Coelogyneae, Coelogyninae)

**Origin** Philippines.

**Description** Medium-sized plant. The pseudobulbs are conical, very close together, 1–1½ in (2–4 cm) long. The leaves are apical, oblanceolate or elliptic, erect, coriaceous, stalked, 6–16 in (15–40 cm) long and 1–1½ in (2–4 cm) wide. The inflorescence is apical, curved, dense, consisting of numerous small flowers among conspicuous straw-colored bracts, and measures up to 20 in (50 cm) long. The small yellow-white flowers open almost simultaneously in winter or early spring.

**Cultivation** This species can be grown either in a pot or a basket of proportional size, with any kind of compost; if bark is used, it is best to enrich it with osmunda fiber or sphagnum. *Dendrochilum* species are popular among growers for their chain of flowers, which bloom in great abundance on well-developed plants. Watering must be frequent during the growth of new vegetation, then slightly reduced. It is advisable, in order to obtain plenty of flowers, not to divide the plants but to let them branch as freely as possible.

## 49 DISA UNIFLORA Berg.
(Diseae, Disinae)

**Synonyms** *Disa barellii* Puydt., *D. grandiflora* L.f., *Satyrium grandiflorum* (L.f.) Thunb.

**Origin** South Africa.

**Description** Medium-sized terrestrial plant, lacking pseudobulbs, with thick roots. The unbranched stem, averaging 20 in (50 cm) in height, comes from a basal rosette. The lanceolate, pointed leaves, 3–8 in (7–20 cm) long, become bracteate toward the tip of the stem. The flowers, borne on the stem apex, seldom number more than 4–5 and have a characteristic form: the sepals, in fact, are the most conspicuous parts whereas the petals and lip are very small. The flowers are generally in various tones of orange, but other colors, such as white, yellow, pink and red, are in great demand. The orchid flowers in spring and summer.

**Cultivation** The *Disa* species are usually considered difficult plants to grow. *D. uniflora* can be raised in a pot using a peat and perlite mix enriched by sphagnum, or even in bark, but again with sphagnum, particularly on the surface. Watering should be regular to maintain plenty of moisture during the growing period which is almost continuous.

## 50 DORITIS PULCHERRIMA Lindl.
(Vandeae, Sarcanthinae)

**Synonym** *Phalaenopsis esmeralda* Rchb. f.

**Origin** Indochinese peninsula and Sumatra.

**Description** Small-medium plant, monopodial in structure. The leaves are alternate, stiff, elliptic, 4–6 in (10–15 cm) long, gray-green flushed with violet especially on the lower side and margin. The inflorescence, which sprouts from the leaf axil, is about 20 in (50 cm) long and bears purple flowers about 1 in (2–3 cm) across. These open in succession so that the plant remains in bloom for many weeks. The petals and sepals are slightly reflexed and the trilobed lip, which has a disk veined in white or yellow, has a small callus. The variety *buyssoniana*, tetraploid, has bigger flowers of a deeper color. An adult plant may produce more than one inflorescence at the same time. The flowering period ranges from late summer to early winter.

**Cultivation** This orchid may be grown either in a pot, on a raft of tree fern or on cork; experience suggests, however, that a pot gives best results. Growing techniques are similar in every respect to those for *Phalaenopsis* (see entry number 120).

**Hybrids** *D. pulcherrima*, the only species of the genus, is widely used for hybridization, especially with *Phalaenopsis* ( = *Doritaenopsis*); it is used for endowing hybrids with particularly attractive violet tints; these may, nevertheless, be masked or even entirely lost in subsequent crosses with *Phalaenopsis* or other colors. Particularly interesting primary hybrids that are easy to obtain include *Doritaenopsis* Bonita (× *stuartiana*), Purple Gem (× *equestris*), Jim Chan (× *amboinensis*), Tan Swee (× *gigantea*), Sweet Gem (× *lueddemenniana*), Kenneth Schubert (× *violacea*), etc.

## 51 DRACULA ERYTHROCHAETE (Rchb. f.) Luer
(Epidendreae, Pleurothallidinae)

**Synonyms** *Masdevallia astuta* Rchb. f., *M. erythrochaete* Rchb. f.
**Origin** From Costa Rica to Colombia.
**Description** Small-medium plant without pseudobulbs. The erect, oblanceolate leaves, about 8 in (20 cm) long, are extremely close together on the rhizome, thus forming small clumps. The slender, pendulous flowering stem, about 6 in (15 cm) long, bears 1–2 flowers that open in slow succession, one at a time. The flowers are triangular, creamy white, with reddish markings and have sepals covered with thick down which extend at the tip into tails measuring several inches in length. The orchid flowers in spring and summer.
**Cultivation** The species should be grown in a small hanging basket so that the inflorescences can trail out in all directions; to achieve this, the compost should be formed into a small mound above the rim of the container. *Dracula* species enjoy a very moist, cool, airy and shady environment; too much water is especially harmful because it may provoke the development of root rot, to which these plants are particularly prone. Repotting is best carried out only when the compost seems to be absorbing an excess of water, and division when the plant has completely filled the container.

---

## 52 DRYADELLA ZEBRINA (Porsch) Luer
(Epidendreae, Pleurothallidinae)

**Synonym** *Masdevallia zebrina* Porsch.
**Origin** Brazil.
**Description** Small plant without pseudobulbs that forms small tufts. The leaves, about 2½ in (6 cm) long, are elliptic-lanceolate, erect, coriaceous and stalked, each on a stem that sprouts from a thin, much-branched rhizome. The flower stem, shorter than the leaves, bears a single greenish, spotted flower of about 1 in (2 cm), the sepal tips of which are lengthened into three characteristic tails. The orchid flowers in spring and summer.
**Cultivation** This species may be grown either in small pots, with very small pieces of bark enriched with osmunda fiber or sphagnum, or on small rafts of tree fern, with clumps of sphagnum placed over the slender roots. The species is rather delicate and cannot endure surroundings that are too hot and dry. Frequent spraying in warm weather helps to encourage development of the plants which, properly cared for, produce large numbers of flowers.

## 53 ENCYCLIA COCHLEATA (L. ) Lemée
(Epidendreae, Laeliinae)

**Synonym** *Epidendrum cochleatum* L.
**Origin** Central America, West Indies, Colombia, Venezuela, Florida.
**Description** Plant of variable size. The pseudobulbs are ovoid and somewhat compressed from side to side, 2–8 in (5–20 cm) long, with 2–3 leaves at the apex. The leaves are elliptic-lanceolate, flexible, 8–12 in (20–30 cm) long and about 2 in (5 cm) wide. The apical inflorescence grows gradually longer over a number of months and easily exceeds 20 in (50 cm); during that period the pale green flowers open in succession, usually 2–3 at a time. They are fairly large and conspicuous, with a characteristically concave, very dark purple lip which, in some specimens, may appear almost black.
**Cultivation** This species is easy to grow, preferably in a pot proportional to the plant's size. The medium can be either bark or osmunda, ideally chopped into small or medium-sized pieces. Watering should be regular throughout the year. Repotting need present no problems.

---

## 54 ENCYCLIA MACULOSA (A.H.S.) Hoehne
(Epidendreae, Laeliinae)

**Synonym** *Epidendrum maculosum* A.H.S.
**Origin** Mexico.
**Description** Medium-sized plant. The pseudobulbs are more or less fusiform, set apart on the rhizome, 2–5 in (15–12 cm) tall, with 2–3 elliptic-ligulate, coriaceous leaves at the apex, 2½–10 in (6–25 cm) long and about 1 in (2 cm) wide. The apical, erect inflorescence, usually more than 4 in (10 cm) long, is made up of a variable number of long-lasting flowers, which open in succession. The flowers, about 1 in (2 cm) across, vary in color from pale to dark brown. Characteristic of the species is the outer surface of the sepals which is covered with papillae. The orchid flowers in spring and summer.
**Cultivation** *E. maculosa* should be grown in medium-sized pots. The recommended growing medium is bark, although the plant adapts to other mixtures. Once the new vegetation is completely developed, the medium should be allowed to dry out between waterings. Repotting and division of this species and others of the same genus should normally be carried out every third year.

## 55 ENCYCLIA MARIAE (Ames) Hoehne
(Epidendreae, Laeliinae)

**Origin** Mexico.
**Description** Medium-small plant. The pseudobulbs are ovoid, about 1½ in (4 cm) tall, with 2–3 apical, grayish-green, elliptic leaves, 4–8 in (10–20 cm) long and about 1 in (2–3 cm) wide. The apical inflorescence is curved, about 6 in (15 cm) long and composed of 2–4 showy, long-lasting flowers that are pale green with a showy white lip and are quite big in relation to the size of the plant. The orchid flowers in summer.
**Cultivation** This species, like most of those that belong to this genus, is easy to cultivate and is recommended even to beginners. The plant can be grown in a pot, in a basket with any type of compost, or on a slab of cork oak bark. Regular watering during the growth period should subsequently be reduced, and followed by a dry period during winter.

## 56 ENCYCLIA VITELLINA (Lindl.) Dressler
(Epidendreae, Laeliinae)

**Synonym** *Epidendrum vitellinum* Lindl.
**Origin** Costa Rica, Guatemala, Mexico.
**Description** Medium-small plant. The pseudobulbs are ovoid, 1–2 in (3–5 cm) tall, and bear at the apex 1–3 erect, elliptic-lanceolate leaves, 4–8 in (10–20 cm) long and ½–1 in (1–2 cm) wide. The erect apical inflorescence, 8–12 in (20–30 cm) long, is sometimes branched and is composed of about a dozen flowers. These are elegantly shaped, showy, long-lasting, measuring about 1 in (3 cm) across, and fairly deep orange in color, all of which attributes make them much prized by collectors. The orchid flowers in autumn and winter.
**Cultivation** *E. vitellina* should be grown in a small pot with fairly light, well-drained compost that does not retain too much moisture. After the complete growth of a new pseudobulb it is best to reduce watering, allowing the medium to dry out almost completely between applications.

## 57 EPIDENDRUM CILIARE L.
(Epidendreae, Laeliinae)

**Origin** Central America, northern parts of South America, West Indies.

**Description** Medium-large plant. The rhizome, always visible, produces pseudobulbs set wide apart, which when mature are cylindrical-fusiform, 6–10 in (15–25 cm) tall. The leaves, generally 1–2 and rarely 3, are borne at the apex of the pseudobulb, and are coriaceous, stiff, lanceolate, 4–12 in (10–30 cm) long. The apical flower stem, about 12 in (30 cm) long, has a series of characteristic imbricate bracts on its lower section and bears a variable number of long-lasting flowers, about 4 in (10 cm) across. These range from white to yellow-green and have a lip that is invariably white, sometimes markedly fringed and voluminous. The orchid flowers in winter.

**Cultivation** This plant is easy to grow and increases rapidly. As a rule it is advisable to repot and divide it every third year to control its size; these operations present no problems.

## 58 EPIDENDRUM CRISTATUM Ruiz et Pavon
(Epidendreae, Laeliinae)

**Synonym** *Epidendrum raniferum* Lindl.

**Origin** Central America, northern parts of South America.

**Description** Large plant without pseudobulbs. The cylindrical stems normally grow to a height of over 3 ft (1 m). The leaves are alternate, coriaceous but flexible, elliptic-lanceolate, persistent for many years to the base of the stem, 6–8 in (15–20 cm) long. The terminal, pendulous inflorescence, 8–12 in (20–30 cm) long, is made up of numerous flowers that open almost simultaneously. They are long-lasting, measure about 1½ in (4 cm) and are yellow-green with a fairly dense and abundant sprinkling of purple spots. The orchid flowers in summer.

**Cultivation** This plant, if properly cared for, increases rapidly, forming large specimens. It is essential to grow it in a big pot because the fairly thick roots grow fast. Bark is the recommended growing medium. Watering should be regular all year round. The species can also be grown in a hothouse without any effect on its vegetational development and flowering potential.

## 59   EPIDENDRUM IBAGUENSE H.B.K.
(Epidendreae, Laeliinae)

**Synonyms** *Epidendrum fulgens* Brongn., *E. radicans* Pavon et Lindl.

**Description** Large plant without pseudobulbs. The slender, upright stems normally grow to a height of over 3 ft (1 m) and bear numerous coriaceous, elliptic, alternate leaves, well separated, about 4 in (10 cm) long and 1½ in (3.5 cm) wide. The apical flower stem easily exceeds 2 ft (60 cm) in length and bears at its tip a dense inflorescence. The individual flowers, which open in succession, are long-lasting and vary considerably in color and size. The species *E. ibaguense* is sometimes confused with *E. secundum* and *E. imatophyllum*, but differs from these in the shape of lip and callus. It flowers at different times of year for many months and is sometimes constantly in bloom.

**Cultivation** This plant, extremely easy to grow, is widely collected. It is generally raised in a pot proportional to its size and adapts to any kind of compost, although bark is usually recommended. It is advisable to attach the long, slender stems to a support. The plant branches freely and abundantly. Like other related species, it adapts well even to environmental conditions not indicated here, and is therefore widely found in all tropical zones as a garden plant. As a rule the stem throws out lateral shoots at varying heights and these root plentifully; they can be detached from the mother plant and repotted to make new specimens.

**Hybrids** *Epiphronitis* Veitchii (*E. ibaguense* × *Sophronitis coccinea* (Lindl.) Rchb. f.) was the first hybrid obtained by using this species, produced in 1890. The plant is similar to *E. ibaguense* but smaller; in fact, the stems are as a rule only 8–12 in (20–30 cm) long, and it tends to grow less vigorously and to look somewhat stunted. The flowers, however, are bigger, better shaped and more deeply colored. The system for growing the hybrid is similar to that employed for the species. The flowers of *Epiphronitis* Veitchii are illustrated in the lower photograph.

Above: *Epidendrum ibaguense*
Below: *Epiphronitis* Veitchii

## 60  EPIDENDRUM PARKINSONIANUM HK.
(Epidendreae, Laeliinae)

**Origin** Central America.

**Description** Large plant of drooping habit with a freely branching rhizome. The pseudobulbs are cylindrical, curved, 3 in (6–8 cm) long, with a single apical leaf which is very fleshy, pendulous and narrowly lanceolate, 10–14 in (25–35 cm) long. The apical inflorescence, several inches long, is produced by the newly formed pseudobulb and is made up of 1–3 large, long-lasting, very showy flowers with a long ovary. The flowers are greenish yellow and have a white lip that is greenish at the apex. They open at different periods of the year, whenever new pseudobulbs appear, most frequently from spring to summer.

**Cultivation** The species, because of its habit, should be grown either on cork or in a hanging basket, preferably on bark, although any other growing medium will do. Watering needs to be regular throughout the year; slightly less frequent for specimens grown on cork. Although the plant branches freely and abundantly, it should not normally be divided because these sections are slow to root.

## 61  EPIDENDRUM PURPURASCENS Focke
(Epidendreae, Laeliinae)

**Synonym** *Epidendrum clavatum* Lindl.

**Origin** Central America, northern parts of South America.

**Description** Medium-sized plant. The club-shaped pseudobulbs, very close together on the rhizome, are about 12 in (30 cm) tall and bear 2–3 horizontal, coriaceous, lanceolate leaves, about 6 in (15 cm) long and 2 in (6 cm) wide, at their apex. The upper quarter of the flower stem, which may grow to a height of more than 32 in (80 cm), bears a variable number of greenish-white flowers about 1½ in (3–4 cm) in diameter, which are long-lasting and open in slow succession. The orchid flowers in winter.

**Cultivation** This species should be grown in small to medium pots, notwithstanding the very long, stiff flowering stems that tend to destabilize the plant. *E. purpurascens* is easy to cultivate and adapts to any compost. It increases slowly. After flowering, a new shoot sprouts from the part of the stem that bore the flowers, and this can be separated from the mother plant as soon as the roots are sufficiently long. When new plant growth is complete, reduce watering slightly.

## 62 ERIA HYACINTHOIDES (Bl.) Lindl.
(Epidendreae, Eriinae)

**Synonym** *Dendrobium hyacinthoides* Bl.
**Origin** Indonesia, Malaysia.
**Description** Medium-sized plant. The pseudobulbs are ovoid, almost spherical, about 3 in (7 cm) tall, sheathed by a number of bractiform, coriaceous leaves, that are apical, erect, lanceolate and coriaceous, about 10 in (25 cm) long. The inflorescence, 1–2 per pseudobulb, subterminal, dense, erect and pubescent, about 6 in (15 cm) long, is made up of many long-lasting flowers about ½ in (1 cm) across. These are white flushed to a varying extent with lilac. The plant in flower looks surprisingly like a small hyacinth. It blooms in spring and summer.
**Cultivation** This species may be grown either in a basket or in a fairly shallow pot. The recommended growing medium is bark enriched by osmunda fiber or sphagnum. Watering, abundant during the growth period, should then be reduced, without allowing the compost to dry out completely. Repotting and division should be carried out only in case of real need.

## 63 ESMERALDA CLARKEI Rchb. f.
(Vandeae, Sarcanthinae)

**Synonyms** *Arachnis clarkei* (Rchb. f.) J.J. Smith, *Arachnanthe clarkei* (Rchb. f.) Rolfe.
**Origin** China, Himalayas, Thailand.
**Description** Plant with a slender, cylindrical stem, generally upright but sometimes curved, up to 3 ft (1 m) long. The coriaceous, ligulate leaves, unequally bilobed at the tip, and about 6 in (15 cm) long, are well separated. The axillary, erect inflorescence, about 12 in (30 cm) long, comprises 4–5 long-lasting, waxy flowers. They are pale to deep yellow, with transverse reddish-brown bars. The orchid usually flowers from late summer to autumn.
**Cultivation** The plant is easy to grow but flowering depends on its being given warm, airy surroundings with plenty of humidity and maximum light – not always easily obtainable outside its natural environment. It is best grown in a pot and adapts to any light, well-drained compost.

## 64 EULOPHIA GUINEENSIS Lindl.
(Cymbidieae, Cyrtopodiinae)

**Origin** Tropical Africa.

**Description** Terrestrial plant of medium-large size. The pseudobulbs, close together on the rhizome, are ovoid, about 2 in (5 cm) long. The large leaves, about 10 in (25 cm) long and 3 in (8 cm) wide, are lanceolate and slightly undulate with very prominent veining, with a petiole that enfolds the upper part of the pseudobulb. The basal flowering stem, about 16 in (40 cm) high, bears at least 10 clustered pink flowers, 1½ in (3–4 cm) across, which open in succession. The orchid flowers from autumn to winter.

**Cultivation** An easily grown plant that needs a rest period of at least one month after the complete development of the pseudobulbs. It is best to repot it every year in medium pots, using bark enriched with sphagnum or osmunda fiber.

## 65 GALEANDRA BAUERI Lindl.
(Cymbidieae, Cyrtopodiinae)

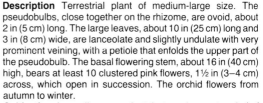

**Origin** Central America.

**Description** Medium-sized plant. The pseudobulbs are fusiform, elongated, close together on the rhizome, at least 10 in (25 cm) tall. There are generally 8 leaves, linear-lanceolate, pointed, coriaceous yet flexible, alternate and set wide apart, sheathing the pseudobulb, about 8 in (20 cm) long and about 1 in (2 cm) wide, with prominent veining. The inflorescence is apical, curved, often branched, fairly lax, about 4 in (10 cm) long. It consists of a few flowers that open in succession and are characteristically funnel-shaped, with a yellow, brown and purple lip, the margin of which is slightly wrinkled with a spur. The orchid flowers in spring.

**Cultivation** This species is usually grown in medium-small, well-drained pots, the compost being a mixture of finely ground bark and sphagnum. Good results can also be obtained by using osmunda or tree-fern fiber. During the growing period the plants should be placed in a very well-lighted position and watered plentifully and frequently. Later there should be a period of partial rest at a lower temperature, with less water given until vegetative growth recommences. Standing water is especially harmful to newly developing shoots.

## 66 GASTROCHILUS BELLINUS (Rchb. f.) O. Ktze.
(Vandeae, Sarcanthinae)

**Synonym** *Saccolabium bellinum* Rchb. f.
**Origin** Burma, Thailand.
**Description** Medium-sized monopodial plant, generally with a shortened stem. The oblanceolate leaves, unequally bilobed at the apex, rather coriaceous, sheathing the stem, are 8–12 in (20–30 cm) long and 1 in (2–3 cm) wide. The very short axillary inflorescence bears a clustered group of small but long-lasting flowers. The triangular lip, fringed at the edge, has long hairs near the base. The orchid flowers from winter to spring.
**Cultivation** The plant can be grown either in a small pot, in a basket, on cork or on a raft. The growing medium, as for all other small and medium-size species, should be made up of small pieces of material. Watering should be regular throughout the year.

---

## 67 GOMESA RECURVA R. Br.
(Cymbidieae, Oncidiinae)

**Synonym** *Rodriguezia recurva* (R. Br.) Lindl.
**Origin** Brazil.
**Description** Medium-sized plant. The pseudobulbs are ovoid, very compressed, close together on the rhizome, displaying longitudinal grooves with age, about 3 in (7 cm) tall, with 2–3 apical leaves, linear-oblanceolate, coriaceous but flexible, 6–12 in (15–30 cm) long and 1 in (2–3 cm) wide. The dense basal inflorescence, curving or pendulous, is 8–12 in (20–30 cm) long. The flowers are quite small and inconspicuous, yellow-green, long-lasting, with parts less wrinkled than in *G. crispa* (Lindl.) Klotzsch ex Rchb. f., from which it differs in having lateral sepals that are joined for over half their length. The orchid flowers from spring to autumn, usually in summer.
**Cultivation** It is best to grow this species in small pots, using any type of well-drained growing medium, in shady, moist surroundings. Watering, frequent during the growth period, should later be reduced a little without allowing the compost to dry out entirely. Repotting should be carried out only when the compost shows signs of disintegrating.

## 68 GONGORA TRUNCATA Lindl.
(Cymbidieae, Stanhopeinae)

**Synonym** *Gongora donckelaariana Lem.*
**Origin** Mexico.
**Description** Medium-large plant. The pseudobulbs are pyriform, fairly deeply grooved, very close together, about 4 in (10 cm) long and with 2 leaves at the apex. The oblanceolate leaves have prominent veins and are coriaceous, stalked, 10–16 in (25–40 cm) long and 3–3½ in (7–9 cm) wide. The inflorescence, sometimes more than one, stems from the base of the pseudobulb and is lax, pendulous, more than 20 in (50 cm) in length. The flowers, about 1½ in (4 cm) in diameter, are straw-colored and purple-spotted. They have a waxy, compressed lip, typically positioned above the column. They open almost simultaneously and last about 2 weeks. The orchid flowers in spring and summer.
**Cultivation** Gongoras are quite easy to grow. They increase rapidly. It is best to raise them in a basket, although they can also be grown in a pot. The medium may consist of bark, osmunda fiber or sphagnum, and must be kept moist during the growth period, slightly less so after the plant has completed its development.

## 69 HELCIA SANGUINOLENTA Lindl.
(Cymbidieae, Oncidiinae)

**Origin** Colombia, Ecuador.
**Description** Medium-sized plant with ovoid, elongated pseudobulbs, 3 in (7–8 cm) tall, that grow very close to the rhizome. The single elongated, elliptic, coriaceous leaves, with an undulate margin, are 4–8 in (10–20 cm) long and 1–2 in (3–5 cm) wide. The many, single-flowered inflorescences appear simultaneously from the base of the plant. The flower, about 2½ in (6 cm) across, is long-lasting and very showy, with its brown-spotted, yellowish-green sepals and petals and white lip. The orchid flowers in winter.
**Cultivation** The species, which comes from the mountains, appreciates cool, humid conditions with abundant watering during plant growth. After complete development it is a good idea to give it a rest period of several weeks to enable the new pseudobulbs to mature.

## 70 HUNTLEYA MELEAGRIS Lindl.
(Maxillariea, Zygopetalinae)

**Synonyms** *Batemania burtii* Endres et Rchb. f., *Zygopetalum meleagris* (Lindl.) Benth.
**Origin** Brazil, Guyana, Venezuela.
**Description** Medium-sized plant without pseudobulbs. The flexible, lanceolate, elongated leaves are tightly imbricate in the form of a fan, measuring 8–10 in (20–25 cm) long. The axillary, upright inflorescence, shorter than the leaves, has a single flat, waxy flower of long duration. The color is very variable but is always in shades of yellow, brown and red. The orchid flowers in summer and autumn.
**Cultivation** Best results are obtained by growing this species in small pots with a light compost of bark mixed with sphagnum or osmunda fiber to maintain adequate moisture. It is important to ensure that no water is left standing in the leaf axil or in the growing medium since the long, thin roots are likely to rot if there is too much water. A freely branched specimen can be divided, but this operation, like repotting, should be done only when new roots begin to sprout.

## 71 IONOPSIS UTRICULARIOIDES (Sw.) Lindl.
(Cymbidieae, Oncidiinae)

**Synonyms** *Epidendrum utricularioides* Sw., *Ionopsis paniculata* Lindl.
**Origin** Tropical and subtropical regions of America.
**Description** Generally a small plant although some specimens may grow to a height of 8–12 in (20–30 cm). The pseudobulbs, ellipsoid, compressed, about ½ in (1 cm) long, occasionally bear a single leaf at the apex but as a rule have none; a further 2–3 linear or lanceolate leaves, carinate, stiff and imbricate, 1–6 in (3–15 cm) sprout from the base of the rhizome, enfolding it. The basal, erect, branched inflorescence, long in relation to the plant's size, is made up of numerous small flowers that open in succession. They range from white to pink, lavender and purple, and have small sepals and petals, while the bilobed lip is broadly expanded. The orchid flowers from winter to spring.
**Cultivation** The species is rather delicate and therefore needs expert handling. It can be grown on a raft but, because the slender, fragile roots must never dry out, it is better to raise it in a small pot with light, finely crumbled bark mixed with sphagnum.

## 72  JUMELLEA SAGITTATA H. Perr.
(Vandeae, Angraecinae)

**Origin** Madagascar.

**Description** Large plant. The leaves are tightly imbricate, linear, unequally bilobed with a dentate apical margin, coriaceous, about 12 in (30 cm) long. The adult plants lose their lower leaves. There are usually many axillary flower stems, 4 in (9–10 cm) long, each bearing one sparkling white flower with a spur measuring 2–2½ in (5–6 cm), and lasting about 10 days. The orchid flowers in spring.

**Cultivation** This species, like many other Angraecinae, is easy to cultivate and grows freely, forming large specimens. It can be raised either in a pot or in a basket in any kind of growing medium, provided it is light and well drained. Watering should be regular throughout the year, although slightly reduced after full development. Repotting presents no problems but should be done only when necessary.

---

## 73  KINGIDIUM DELICIOSUM (Rchb. f.) Sweet
(Vandeae, Sarcanthinae)

**Synonyms** *Kingiella decumbens* (Griff.) P.H. Hunt, *Phalaenopsis deliciosa* Rchb. f.

**Origin** India, Sri Lanka, Southeast Asia.

**Description** Small plant with monopodial structure. The base of the very short stem is completely sheathed by 4–5 obovate leaves with undulate margins, slightly fleshy, 4–6 in (10–15 cm) long. The axillary inflorescences, branched, erect or curved, about 4 in (10 cm) long, are composed of numerous small lilac flowers that open in succession. The plant freely throws out side shoots. The general appearance resembles a small *Phalaenopsis*. The orchid flowers at various times of the year, but especially in summer.

**Cultivation** The plant requires no particular attention but, as in the case of *Phalaenopsis* and *Doritis*, no standing water should be allowed to collect around the plant apex. It is best grown in a small pot. In the course of repotting, which needs to be done regularly every other year, plants that have branched to excess may be divided.

## 74 LAELIA FLAVA Lindl.
(Epidendreae, Laeliinae)

**Synonyms** *Laelia fulvia*, Lindl., *Cattleya lutea* Beer.
**Origin** Brazil.
**Description** Medium-sized plant with almost cylindrical pseudobulbs, close together on the rhizome, 4–8 in (10–20 cm) tall, bearing a single lanceolate, fleshy, upright, stiff leaf, green flushed with violet-brown. The inflorescence, 12–16 in (30–40 cm) long, usually has fewer than 10 lemon-yellow flowers, 1 in (3 cm) in diameter, near the tip. The orchid generally flowers in spring.
**Cultivation** *L. flava* is a rupicolous species that can nevertheless adapt to being grown in a pot with bark or tree-fern fiber. During the growth of new vegetation the plant needs regular watering, which should be suspended after complete development for a rest period. Particular care must be taken over repotting, which should be carried out only when absolutely necessary; the species does not tolerate being disturbed.
**Hybrids** See *Cattleya*.

## 75 LAELIA GOULDIANA Rchb. f.
(Epidendreae, Laeliinae)

**Origin** Mexico.
**Description** Medium-sized plant with elongated, pyriform pseudobulbs, about 6 in (15 cm) tall, bearing at the apex 2–3 lanceolate, coriaceous, stiff leaves, about 6 in (15 cm) long. The terminal part of the apical inflorescence, some 8 in (20 cm) in length, has a group of conspicuous, long-lasting purple flowers, 3 in (7–8 cm) in diameter that open almost simultaneously. *L. gouldiana* is sometimes regarded as one of the natural hybrids of *L. autumnalis* and *L. anceps*. The orchid flowers in winter.
**Cultivation** This is one of the easiest laelias to grow. It can be grown either in a basket with bark or osmunda or on blocks of tree fern. The plant, if well cared for, branches freely, forming large specimens. Regular watering should be eased off slightly after the complete development of new growth, especially in the case of specimens grown in pots, so that the compost can dry out slowly.

## 76 LAELIA GRANDIS Lindl.
(Epidendreae, Laeliinae)

**Origin** Brazil.
**Description** Medium-large plant. The fusiform, slightly compressed pseudobulbs are about 8 in (20 cm) tall and bear at the apex a single lanceolate, stiff, coriaceous leaf, about 12 in (30 cm) long and 2 in (5 cm) wide. The inflorescence has 3–5 flowers of 4–5 in (10–12 cm) diameter and emerges from the spathe. The white and purple flowers open all at the same time and last a few days. The undulate petals and sepals, slightly twisted in a spiral, are very characteristic. The orchid flowers in spring.
**Cultivation** This species, like virtually all the Brazilian laelias, needs plenty of light and a fairly high temperature. It is best grown in a pot with bark. It is also advisable, for this and the related *L. purpurata* and *L. tenebrosa*, to reduce watering after complete development of the new growth.

## 77 LAELIA JONGHEANA Rchb. f.
(Epidendreae, Laeliinae)

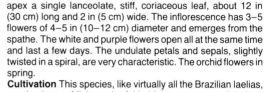
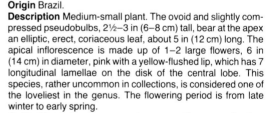

**Origin** Brazil.
**Description** Medium-small plant. The ovoid and slightly compressed pseudobulbs, 2½–3 in (6–8 cm) tall, bear at the apex an elliptic, erect, coriaceous leaf, about 5 in (12 cm) long. The apical inflorescence is made up of 1–2 large flowers, 6 in (14 cm) in diameter, pink with a yellow-flushed lip, which has 7 longitudinal lamellae on the disk of the central lobe. This species, rather uncommon in collections, is considered one of the loveliest in the genus. The flowering period is from late winter to early spring.
**Cultivation** *L. jongheana* may be grown either on a raft or in a pot, with bark, tree-fern fiber or osmunda. If well cultivated, it produces a number of shoots at the same time.

## 78 LEMBOGLOSSUM CERVANTESII (La Llave et Lex.) Halbinger
(Cymbidieae, Oncidiinae)

**Synonyms** *Odontoglossum cervantesii* La Llave et Lex., *O. membranaceum* Lindl.
**Origin** Guatemala, Mexico.
**Description** Medium-sized plant. The ovoid, compressed pseudobulbs, close together on the rhizome, are about 2 in (5 cm) tall and bear at the apex a single elliptic-lanceolate, flexible leaf, 4–6 in (10–15 cm) long and about 1 in (3 cm) wide. The flowering stem, generally 1 but sometimes 2, emerges from the base of the pseudobulb, and is erect or curved, 6–12 in (15–30 cm) long, sheathed at the base by several dry bracts. The flowers, up to 6 per inflorescence, are about 2 in (5 cm) in diameter and vary from white to pink with concentric streaks on sepals and petals; they are long-lasting though delicate. The orchid generally flowers in winter. This orchid and several related species have recently been separated from the genus *Odontoglossum* in which they were formerly described.
**Cultivation** *L. cervantesii* comes from mountain zones above 5,000 ft (1,500 m) and needs to be grown in cool, moist and well-illuminated surroundings. It should be grown in small to medium pots in a light, moist, very well-drained medium. Take care not to over or underwater. A dry period of several months is desirable in winter. Feed with doses half that of a normal application.

---

## 79 LEPANTHES OVALIS (Sw.) Fawc. et Rendle
(Epidendreae, Pleurothallidinae)

**Origin** Cuba, Jamaica.
**Description** Medium-small plant without pseudobulbs. The slender, upright stems, about 8 in (20 cm) long, sprout closely together from a short rhizome and bear a single, elliptic, coriaceous leaf, 1½–3 in (4–7 cm) long and about 1 in (2.5 cm) wide. A number of inflorescences grow from the point where the leaf is inserted on the stem; these are shorter than the leaves themselves and made up of many small yellowish flowers, characteristic in shape, which open in slow succession so that only a few are present simultaneously. The orchid flowers at various times of the year, most frequently in spring.
**Cultivation** *Lepanthes* species usually need handling by experts, as they are rather delicate and are demanding about surrounding conditions, requiring plenty of moisture, good ventilation and a temperature not exceeding 75–77°F (24–25°C). It is best to grow the species illustrated here in small pots, with a compost made up of a mixture of finely chopped bark, sphagnum and osmunda. Watering should be frequent and regular throughout the year.

## 80 LEPTOTES BICOLOR Lindl.
(Epidendreae, Laeliinae)

**Synonym** *Tetramicra bicolor* (Lindl.) Benth.
**Origin** Brazil.
**Description** Plant of modest dimensions which, thanks to its much-branched rhizome, grows freely to form compact plants. The cylindrical pseudobulbs, ½–1 in (1–2 cm) long, bear at their apex a fleshy, subcylindrical, pointed leaf, upright or drooping, dark green, 2–4 in (5–10 cm) long. The inflorescence, erect or curved, is shorter than the leaves and normally comprises 2–4 white and purple flowers measuring 1 in (2–3 cm). These do not always open completely and last a long time. The orchid flowers in late winter.

**Cultivation** *L. bicolor* is usually cultivated on a tree-fern raft where it grows quite prolifically, but it can also be raised in small baskets, in which case the compost should consist of finely chopped bark supplemented by osmunda fiber or sphagnum. When new growth is completed it is advisable to reduce watering without allowing the medium to dry out completely, especially for raft specimens.

## 81 LIPARIS GUINEENSIS Lindl.
(Malaxidae)

**Origin** Tropical West Africa.
**Description** Small-medium terrestrial plant. The leaves, generally 4 in number, sprout from the thickened base of the stem, which they sheathe; they are elliptic, membranous, plicate, stalked and deciduous, about 8 in (20 cm) long and approximately 2½ in (6 cm) wide. The erect inflorescence, longer than the leaves, bears many small, green, yellow, brown or purple flowers, not of long duration, which open in succession. These appear in summer.

**Cultivation** Not often collected *L. guineensis* should be grown in small pots. The ideal medium is a mixture of equal parts of osmunda fiber and sphagnum. This needs to be kept very moist during the growth and development of the inflorescence; at the end of this period watering should be markedly reduced, thus enabling the plant to rest. At this time the leaves become dry. Repotting should be carried out when the compost begins to break up.

## 82 LOCKHARTIA LUNIFERA (Lindl.) Rchb. f.
(Cymbidieae, Oncidiinae)

**Origin** Brazil.

**Description** Medium-small plant without pseudobulbs. The stems are erect, very close together, measuring 4–12 in (10–30 cm) or more in length. The leaves are very numerous, triangular, bilaterally compressed, densely imbricate, about ½ in (1.5 cm) long, arranged all along the stem. The axillary, curved flower stalks, about ¾ in (2 cm) long, spring from the apical portion of the main stem and bear several flowers subtended by a characteristically concave bract. The long-lasting yellow flowers have a typical lip that is deeply trilobed in the form of a saddle. The orchid flowers in spring and summer.

**Cultivation** The *Lockhartia* species may be grown either in a pot or in a basket, using a well-drained medium with plenty of osmunda fiber or sphagnum. Watering should be spaced out so that the growing medium is kept continually moist but not waterlogged, which is particularly harmful to these plants. Repotting should be done only when the compost shows signs of breaking up.

---

## 83 LUDISIA DISCOLOR (Ker-Gawl.) A. Rich.
(Cranichideae, Goodyerinae)

**Synonym** *Haemaria discolor* (Ker-Gawl.) Lindl.

**Origin** India, Indonesia, Indochinese peninsula.

**Description** Medium-small terrestrial plant without pseudobulbs. The fleshy, reddish-brown stems, fairly erect and twisted, are 8–10 in (20–25 cm) long. The attractive leaves, dark reddish-green with pale venation, are elliptic-lanceolate, stalked, 2–3 in (4–7 cm) long and about 1 in (3 cm) wide. The terminal, cylindrical, fairly dense inflorescence, at least 4 in (10 cm) long, bears many small, asymmetrical flowers that are white with yellow on the lip and last about 2 weeks. The orchid flowers in winter.

**Cultivation** This species, together with others that belong to related genera (*Goodyera, Macodes* and *Zeuxine*) is grown principally for its beautiful leaves. *L. discolor* is considered by some to be a difficult plant, but excellent results can be obtained by raising it in small-medium pots or in baskets, in a medium consisting of bark enriched by sphagnum. Watering should keep the growing medium always moist but not waterlogged.

## 84 LYCASTE AROMATICA (Hooker) Lindl.
(Maxillarieae, Lycastinae)

**Synonyms** *Maxillaria aromatica* Hooker, *Lycaste suaveolens* Summerh.
**Origin** Guatemala, Honduras, Mexico.
**Description** Medium-large plant. The pseudobulbs, 3–4 in (7–10 cm) tall, are ovoid, compressed, slightly grooved horizontally and closely grouped on the rhizome. Two or more lanceolate, plicate, membranous, deciduous leaves are borne at the apex of the pseudobulb; they may measure more than 20 in (50 cm) in length and are about 6 in (15 cm) wide. The conspicuous and long-lasting yellow flowers, 3–4 in (7–10 cm) in diameter, arise singly on stalks, about 6 in (15 cm) long, which stem from the base of the pseudobulb. The orchid generally flowers in spring.
**Cultivation** The *Lycaste* species are usually grown in pots proportional to their size, and should be left in these until division is required. These plants require abundant watering while new vegetation is growing, followed by a rest period at a lower temperature, when water is withheld almost completely.

## 85 LYCASTE DEPPEI (Lodd.) Lindl.
(Maxillarieae, Lycastinae)

**Synonym** *Maxillaria deppei* Lodd.
**Origin** Guatemala, Mexico.
**Description** Medium-sized plant. The pseudobulbs are ovoid, slightly compressed, rugose, grooved longitudinally, 2–4 in (5–10 cm) tall, and bear at their apex a number of elliptic-oblanceolate, plicate, membranous, deciduous leaves, 12–16 in (30–40 cm) long and 3–4 in (8–10 cm) wide. The basal, upright flower stems, 4–6 in (10–15 cm) long, are sheathed by various imbricate and swollen bracts; they carry a single large, long-lasting, waxy flower, the sepals of which vary in color from green to yellow, fairly densely covered with small reddish-orange spots. The orchid flowers in spring.
**Cultivation** The *Lycaste* orchids require cool and well-ventilated surroundings; pools of water and still air are particularly harmful. The recommended growing medium is bark supplemented by sphagnum, but good results may also be achieved using osmunda fiber.
**Hybrids** The genus comprises some 25 species, many of which have been widely hybridized both with one another and with species of other closely related genera, to produce clones of extraordinary beauty, such as *Angulocaste* (= *L.* × *Anguloa*), *Lycasteria* (= *L.* × *Bifrenaria*), and *Zygocaste* (= *L.* × *Zygopetalum*).

## 86 MACRADENIA MULTIFLORA (Kraenzl.) Cogn.
(Cymbidieae, Oncidiinae)

**Origin** Brazil.

**Description** Medium-small plant. The pyriform, slightly compressed pseudobulbs are about 2 in (5 cm) tall, close together on the rhizome and fairly dark green; at their apex is a single erect, coriaceous, lanceolate leaf, about 6 in (15 cm) long and about 2 in (5 cm) wide. The basal inflorescence, which is curved, pendulous and dense, is composed of numerous flowers, and measures 6–8 in (15–20 cm) in length. As a rule each new pseudobulb produces two inflorescences. The rather small, very showy and long-lasting, red and yellow flowers have a trilobed, white lip, of which the middle lobe is narrow and elongated like a small tongue, and the outer lobes are pointed and slightly fringed. The orchid flowers in summer and autumn.

**Cultivation** The 15 or so species that belong to this genus are not frequently grown, even though they are quite easy to handle, small in size and free-flowering. These plants can be grown either on a raft of tree fern or cork or in small pots; in the latter case the medium can consist of osmunda, sphagnum, fern fiber, bark or, ideally, a mixture in equal parts of various of these materials. Watering should be regular throughout the year.

---

## 87 MALAXIS LATIFOLIA Sm.
(Malaxideae)

**Synonym** *Microstylis latifolia* J.J.S.

**Origin** Australia, southern China, India, Indochinese peninsula.

**Description** Medium-small terrestrial plant. The pseudobulb gives the impression of being a thickening of the lower part of the stem and is sheathed by the lower portion of the leaf stalk. There are normally 4–5 leaves, elliptic-lanceolate, flexible, plicate, 4–8 in (10–20 cm) long and 1½–2 in (4–5 cm) wide. The fairly dense, erect inflorescence, about 8 in (20 cm) long, is composed of many delicate, small, green or reddish-green flowers, which open in succession. The orchid generally flowers in autumn and winter.

**Cultivation** This species should be cultivated in small pots and, as for the majority of terrestrial orchids from the tropics, the recommended medium is a mixture of osmunda fiber, sphagnum and finely chopped bark, which should always be kept moist. Repotting may be done when the compost, because of age, retains too much water.

## 88 MASDEVALLIA GLANDULOSA Kgr.
(Epidendreae, Pleurothallidinae)

**Origin** Peru.
**Description** Small plant, which like all species of this genus, lacks pseudobulbs. The leaves are more or less elliptic, coriaceous, erect, stalked, about 5 in (13 cm) long and about 1 in (2 cm) wide. The upright flower stem, shorter than the leaves, bears a single flower: sometimes 2–3 stems are produced simultaneously from the same point of leaf insertion. The campanulate flowers have sepals that are of varying shades of purple inside, and are covered with papillae. The appendages, or tails, which lengthen the sepals, measure a few inches in length. The orchid flowers in winter.
**Cultivation** This species, recently described, was found in the mountain regions of Peru; so when cultivated it needs cool, wet, airy surroundings. It is best to grow it in small pots in a light medium enriched with osmunda fiber or sphagnum. Watering should be maintained throughout the year so that the medium is always moist, but care needs to be taken not to overwater since this can cause rotting of roots and stems.

## 89 MASDEVALLIA IGNEA Rchb. f.
(Epidendreae, Pleurothallidinae)

**Synonym** *Masdevallia militaris* Rchb. f.
**Origin** Colombia.
**Description** Medium-small plant that grows freely. The leaves are elliptic-obovate, stalked, erect, coriaceous, slightly carinate, glossy, 8–9 in (20–23 cm) long and about 1 in (3 cm) wide. The flower stem, which is longer than the leaves, is upright and bears a single showy flower, in various shades of orange, red or purple; the dorsal sepal is folded over the lateral sepals and extends into a tail several inches long. The orchid flowers in spring and summer.
**Cultivation** This species from the high mountains of Colombia, enjoys cool, very wet and airy conditions. It needs to be grown in small pots with a well-drained medium containing plenty of sphagnum or osmunda fiber. It is advisable to repot *Masdevallia* species only when the plants are well grown and the compost shows signs of decomposition.

## 90  MASDEVALLIA TRIANGULARIS Lindl.
(Epidendreae, Pleurothallidinae)

**Origin** Colombia, Venezuela.

**Description** Medium-small plant. The leaves, measuring about 6 in (15 cm) long and 1 in (3 cm) wide, are more or less obovate, erect or suberect, coriaceous, stalked, their margin tending to furl toward the base. The erect flower stem, shorter than the leaves, bears a single flower, which is yellow-green with a dense scattering of reddish-brown spots. The sepals, carinate on the back, have characteristic tails about 1 in (4–6 cm) long. The orchid flowers in summer.

**Cultivation** This is another species, fairly widely collected, from the high mountain, tropical forest zones, which demands a cool and airy environment. It should be grown in small pots, and the growing medium enriched with osmunda fiber or sphagnum, always moist but not waterlogged. In warm weather, the *Masdevallia* orchids, in addition to regular watering, benefit from having water sprayed on the leaves and surrounding areas.

## 91  MASDEVALLIA Marguerite
(*M. infracta* Lindl. × *M. veitchiana* Rchb. f.)

The majority of *Masdevallia* orchids are found in the high mountain forest regions of the intertropical belt of Central and South America; this means that when they are cultivated they require a cool, very moist and well-ventilated environment all the year round. Because of these cultural requirements the plants have a reputation of being hard to grow other than by experts who can provide the necessary climatic conditions. A few species do come from warmer regions and may therefore be accommodated in a temperate or intermediate greenhouse. In fairly recent years this genus has been involved in large-scale hybridization, partly using these temperate-greenhouse species to obtain hybrids with less rigorous cultural requirements. The species most frequently used are; *M. infracta, M. strobelii, M. rolfeana, M. angulata, M. gutierrezii* and *M. floribunda*. Many of the clones thus obtained are highly desirable both for the quality and quantity of their flowers and for their vigorous growth habits: *M.* Marguerite is an excellent example of such hybrids.

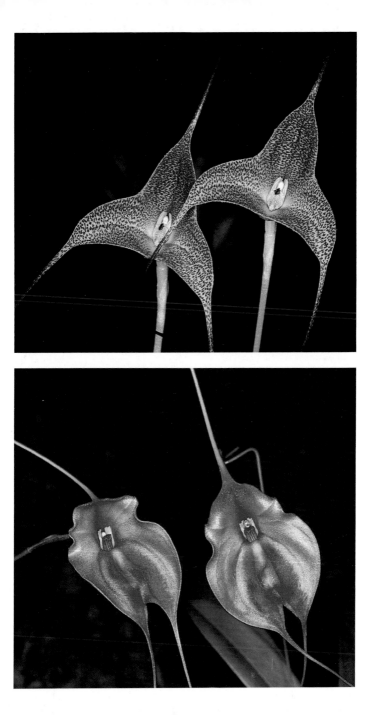

## 92 MAXILLARIA PICTA Hooker
(Maxillarieae, Maxillariinae)

**Synonym** *Maxillaria fuscata* Klotzsch.
**Origin** Eastern Brazil.
**Description** Medium-small plant. The pseudobulbs, 2–3 in (5–7 cm) tall, are pyriform, close together on the rhizome, with longitudinal grooves that become more accentuated with age. The leaves, 1–3 per pseudobulb, are apical, linear-lanceolate, coriaceous yet flexible, 10–14 in (25–35 cm) long and about 1½ in (4 cm) wide. The flower stems, erect or pendulous, sheathed by several bracts, are about 6 in (15 cm) long; they emerge from the base of the pseudobulb and each bears a single campanulate yellow, spotted flower of medium size that lasts about 20 days. The orchid flowers in autumn.
**Cultivation** An easy-to-grow plant that increases rapidly. It can be grown either in a pot or in a basket in various growing media. Watering should be regular throughout the year, but it is advisable to reduce it slightly after the full growth of new vegetation. Repotting and division present no problems, but it is advisable to keep the plant for several years in the same container so as to have an abundance of flowers.

## 93 MAXILLARIA RUFESCENS Lindl.
(Maxillarieae, Maxillariinae)

**Synonym** *Maxillaria acutifolia* Lindl.
**Origin** Central America and northern parts of South America, West Indies.
**Description** Medium-small plant. The pseudobulbs, variable in shape, are usually ellipsoid and rather compressed, bearing at their apex a single elliptic-lanceolate leaf that is erect, coriaceous, about 10 in (25 cm) long and about 1½ in (4 cm) wide. The basal flower stem, usually about 2 in (5 cm) long, bears a single more or less campanulate flower, very conspicuous, varying in color from yellow to deepish orange, with red spots; rarely the flowers may be white or green with a dark red streak. The flowering period is variable and particularly protracted as the numerous flowers appear gradually.
**Cultivation** An easily grown plant, best cultivated in small-medium pots and left to increase before the container is changed. Like the majority of *Maxillaria* species, it adapts to any kind of growing medium.

## 94 MILTONIA Lindl.
(Cymbidieae, Oncidiinae)

**Origin** Andes area, eastern Brazil, Costa Rica, Panama.

**Description** Medium-sized plants. The pseudobulbs, which sprout from the branched rhizome, are 2–4 in (5–10 cm) long, ovoid, compressed, and yellow-green like the leaves. The 2 leaves are apical, linear, pointed and flexible, 8–20 in (20–50 cm) long. The basal, erect inflorescence, 2–20 in (5–50 cm) in length, comprises a variable number of flowers, measuring 2–3 in (5–7 cm) in diameter, differing in color depending on species, long-lasting and opening in succession. The orchid flowers in spring and summer.

**Cultivation** The *Miltonia* species may be grown either in pots or in medium-sized baskets, with a medium that consists essentially of bark with the addition of osmunda fiber or sphagnum. Those species with pseudobulbs spaced well apart on the rhizome are best raised in a basket where they have more room to expand. Watering should be plentiful and frequent during the growing period, then slightly reduced. Recently a small number of species included in the genus *Miltonia* have been reassigned to the genus *Miltoniopsis*. These differ from the original group both in their large flowers, which are sometimes called pansy orchids, in the single leaf at the apex of the pseudobulb, and in cultural requirements; in fact, because they all come from mountain regions, they prefer lower temperatures and more humidity. The *Miltoniopsis* species, furthermore, need to be grown in small well-drained pots with a medium made up of bark that should always be kept moist.

**Hybrids** Both the *Miltonia* and *Miltoniopsis* orchids have been involved in hybridization, either using species only of the one or other genus or crossing each of them with related genera of the same subtribe. The *Miltoniopsis* species, in particular, have been used to obtain especially beautiful and characteristically shaped flowers, while the *Miltonia* species help to produce more brilliantly colored hybrids capable of withstanding higher temperatures.

Opposite above: *Miltonia regnellii*.
Opposite below: *Miltoniopsis* Charlesworthii.

## 95 MORMODES WARSCEWICZII Klotzsch
(Cymbidieae, Catasetinae)

**Synonym** *Mormodes histrio* Linden et Rchb. f.
**Origin** From Mexico to Peru.
**Description** Medium-sized plant. The pseudobulbs, cylindrical-fusiform, with many nodes, are covered with dry, whitish bracts and are 6–8 in (15–20 cm) long. The leaves are elliptic-lanceolate, plicate, membranous, deciduous, measuring about 8 in (20 cm) long and about 1½ in (4 cm) wide. The curved inflorescences, more than one per pseudobulb, are 8–12 in (20–30 cm) long, sprout successively from the nodes and comprise many flowers. These vary in size and color and are characteristically irregular in shape. The orchid flowers from spring to summer.
**Cultivation** The *Mormodes* species, like all the other Catasetinae, are not particularly difficult plants to grow but require a good deal of care in watering, especially after repotting. During this period, the plants should be left completely dry until the new roots start growing plentifully. The plant should be grown either in a pot or a small basket, in any kind of medium. It should be repotted every year.
**Hybrids** Some *Mormodes* species have been hybridized with species belonging to the related genus *Cycnoches* (= *Cycnodes*), thus obtaining interesting clones that appeal particularly to collectors.

---

## 96 NAGELIELLA PURPUREA (Lindl.) L.O. Wms
(Epidendreae, Laeliinae)

**Synonym** *Hartwegia purpurea* Lindl.
**Origin** Guatemala, Honduras, Mexico.
**Description** Medium-small plant. The pseudobulbs are more or less clavate, 1–3 in (2–8 cm) tall; at the apex is a single leaf, erect, coriaceous, lanceolate-ovate, purple-spotted, 1–5 in (3–12 cm) long and about ½ in (1.5 cm) wide. The apical, erect inflorescence, about 16 in (40 cm) long, bears several purple-pink flowers measuring ½ in (1.5 cm) across and opening in succession. The orchid flowers in summer.
**Cultivation** An easily grown plant that can be raised in a small pot or on a tree-fern raft. The recommended medium is osmunda fiber or finely chopped bark. Watering should be frequent enough to keep the mix constantly moist; too much water damages this species. Repotting and division should be carried out only when the plants are well developed. It is best to leave the flowering stems on the plant after blooming in order to obtain flowers in succeeding years.

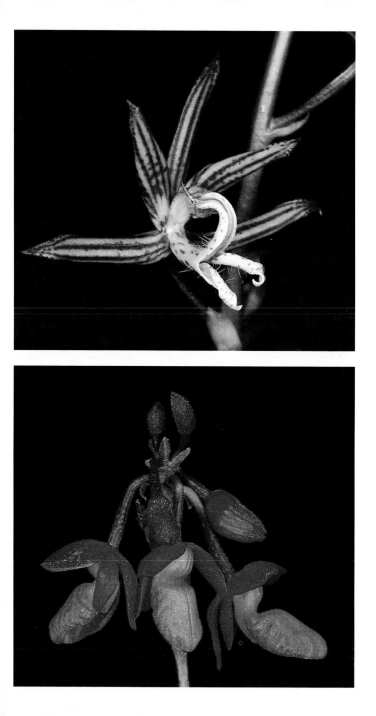

## 97 NEOFINETIA FALCATA (Thunb.) Hu
(Vandeae, Sarcanthinae)

**Synonym** *Angraecum falcatum* (Thunb.) Lindl.
**Origin** Japan, Korea.
**Description** Plant with monopodial habit, branched from base, seldom exceeding 4 in (10 cm) in height. The bright green leaves are alternate, linear, pointed, carinate, stiff, slightly down-curving and tightly imbricate, about 2½ in (6 cm) long. The tips of the inflorescences, about as long as the leaves, bear many completely white flowers furnished with a long, thin and curved spur. Specimens with variegated leaves are especially rare and sought after. The orchid flowers in summer.
**Cultivation** *N. falcata* is best grown in small pots. The growing medium may be bark, sphagnum, osmunda or tree-fern fiber, provided it is well drained and aerated. Repotting is advisable only every other year at most.
**Hybrids** *N. falcata*, which is the only species of the genus, has been hybridized with, among others, *Ascocentrum, Vanda, Phalaenopsis, Aerides* and *Sedirea*; such hybrids, however, are hard to come across, usually being found in specialist collections.

## 98 NOTYLIA BARKERI Lindl.
(Cymbidieae, Oncidiinae)

**Synonyms** *Notylia trisepala* Lindl. et Paxt., *N. bipartita* Rchb. f.
**Origin** Central America.
**Description** Medium-small plant. The pseudobulbs are ellipsoid, compressed, very close together on the rhizome, ½–1 in (1–3 cm) tall; at their apex is a single leaf that is erect, coriaceous, more or less elliptic, 1–6 in (3–15 cm) long and ½–1 in (1–3 cm) wide. The basal inflorescence is pendulous and lax, with many flowers, normally 6–8 in (15–20 cm) long, sometimes even longer. The flowers are small, yellow-green, and open in swift succession. The orchid usually flowers in spring.
**Cultivation** This is a rather delicate species that should be grown in small pots or on a tree-fern raft. In the latter case it needs frequent watering in order to prevent the medium from drying out, especially during the growth period. If grown in a pot, use fine bark with an addition of sphagnum. Repotting should be done only when necessary.

## 99 ODONTOGLOSSUM CRISPUM Lindl.
(Cymbidieae, Oncidiinae)

**Synonym** *Odontoglossum alexandrae* Batem.
**Origin** Colombia.
**Description** Medium-sized plant. The pseudobulbs are ovoid, compressed, about 2½ in (6 cm) tall, quite closely grouped on the rhizome, with 2 leaves at the apex. The leaves are linear-lanceolate, fairly coriaceous and flexible, 12–16 in (30–40 cm) long and about 1 in (3 cm) wide; after 2–3 years they may drop. The inflorescences, sometimes 2 per pseudobulb, basal, erect, curved or pendulous, 16–24 in (40–60 cm) long, are as a rule composed of many flowers arranged in a loose spike. Variable in shape, colored white with a pink flush and few or many brown or purple spots, they open in succession and last a long time. The orchid usually flowers in winter.
**Cultivation** The species originates in mountain areas above 6,500 ft (2,000 m) and so requires cool, moist, airy and well-lighted surroundings. These plants should be grown in relatively small pots, with a growing medium that is moist but not soaked. Too much watering may provoke rotting, while too little causes curling of new shoots and eventual death of the whole plant.
**Hybrids** This species of *Odontoglossum* is more widely used for hybridization than any other of the genus because of the extraordinary beauty of its flowers. It appears in the family tree of many of the finest clones.

## 100 ODONTOGLOSSUM MACULATUM La Llave et Lex.
(Cymbidieae, Oncidiinae)

**Synonym** *Lemboglossum* (La Llave et Lex.) Halbinger.
**Origin** Guatemala, Mexico.
**Description** Medium-sized plant. The pseudobulbs are ovoid, compressed, 1½–3½ in (4–9 cm) tall, and bear at the apex 1–2 elliptic-lanceolate, coriaceous yet fairly flexible leaves, 4–12 in (10–30 cm) long and 1–2 in (2–5 cm) wide. The inflorescence is basal, upright or pendulous, lax, sometimes branched, and its length depends on the number of flowers, generally exceeding 12 in (30 cm). The conspicuous, long-lasting flowers, which open in succession, have yellow-green petals with brown spots. The orchid normally flowers in summer.
**Cultivation** This species, like the other species from Mexico, formerly classified in *Odontoglossum*, comes from the high mountains and therefore needs temperatures of not more than 75–77°F (24–25°C), high humidity and plenty of air. It should be grown in fairly small, well-drained pots, with compost that is moist but not waterlogged in summer and allowed to dry out between waterings in winter. Repotting and division should be effected, after flowering, when the plants are well developed.
**Note** Recent studies have shown that all the Mexican species of *Odontoglossum* should now be included in the genus *Lemboglossum* Halbinger.

## 101 ODONTOCIDIUM Tiger Hambühren
*(Oncidium maculatum* Lindl. × *Odontoglossum* Goldrausch)

The hybrids obtained by crossing various *Odontoglossum* species are often highly floriferous plants with particularly beautiful flowers that are sometimes sold by florists; but they may be difficult to cultivate, in particular because they need cool summer temperatures. With a view to eliminating or at least reducing these problems, growers have crossed the floriferous species of *Odontoglossum* with species of related genera (ie., *Oncidium, Miltonia* and *Brassia*), that tolerate a wider range of growing conditions, often obtaining very beautiful clones that are sought both by florists and collectors: *Vuylstekeara* (= *Odontoglossum* × *Cochlioda* × *Miltonia*), *Wilsonara* (*Odontoglossum* × *Cochlioda* × *Oncidium*), *Sanderara* (*Odontoglossum* × *Brassia* × *Cochlioda*), *Odontonia* (*Odontoglossum* × *Miltonia*), *Colmanara* (*Odontoglossum* × *Miltonia* × *Oncidium*), etc. *Odontocidium* Tiger Hambühren is certainly a fine example of all this activity!

A luxuriant plant, which grows rapidly, it produces 2 branched flowering stems to each 8–12 in (20–30 cm) pseudobulb. The plant bears numerous conspicuous and long-lasting, yellow and brown flowers measuring 3 in (7–8 cm) in diameter. It can be grown in the coolest part of the greenhouse.

---

## 102 OECEOCLADES MACULATA (Lindl.) Lindl.
(Cymbidieae, Cyrtopodiinae)

**Synonym** *Eulophidium maculatum* (Lindl.) Pfitz.
**Origin** Intertropical areas of the Americas and Africa.
**Description** Medium-small terrestrial plant. The pseudobulbs, about 1 in (2.5 cm) tall, are ovoid, slightly compressed, and situated close together on the rhizome, with a single leaf at the apex. The leaf is almost elliptic, suberect, coriaceous, marbled in various shades of green, 8 in (20 cm) long and about 2½ in (6 cm) wide. The lax, basal, erect inflorescences are 12–16 in (30–40 cm) long. There are sometimes 2 per pseudobulb. They are made up of a variable number of small flowers, ranging from white to brown or pink. This orchid flowers in autumn, but is sometimes disappointing when the flowers are self-pollinated and fade quickly.
**Cultivation** An easy-to-grow plant that should be kept in a pot proportional to its size. It is best to use a medium consisting of equal parts of bark and sphagnum. (The sphagnum may be replaced, by osmunda or leafmold). Watering should be regular throughout the year but slightly reduced during the period when there is no active plant growth. Repotting should be done after flowering or when the medium starts to break down.

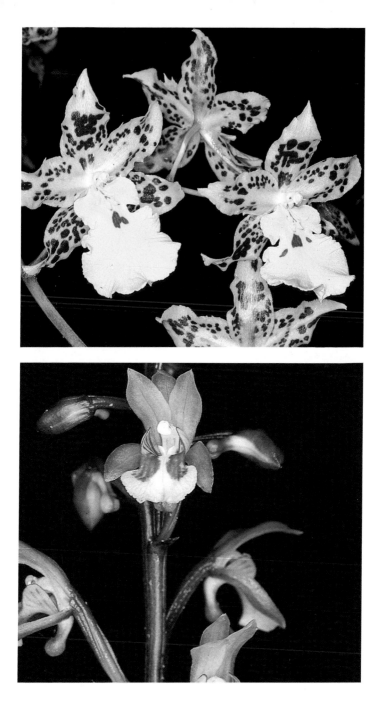

## 103    ONCIDIUM CEBOLLETA (Jacq.) Sw.
(Cymbidieae, Oncidiinae)

**Synonym** *Dendrobium cebolleta* Jacq.
**Origin** Intertropical America.
**Description** Medium-sized plant. The small, barely distin-guishable pseudobulbs, covered by dry bracts, are grouped closely together on the rhizome. The leaves, one per pseudobulb, are cylindrical, grooved, pointed, stiff, erect or pendulous, green-brown with purple spots, measuring 4–16 in (10–40 cm) long and about ½ in (1 cm) in diameter. The basal, stiff, branched inflorescence is pendulous or erect and gener-ally measures 8–12 in (20–30 cm), although in especially vig-orous plants it may reach a length of 3 ft (1 m). It is made up of numerous highly conspicuous and long-lasting yellow and brown flowers that open all together and are about 1 in (2 cm) in diameter. The orchid flowers from late winter to spring.
**Cultivation** This species is best grown on a tree-fern raft. Abundant and frequent watering during the growth period should be much reduced later. The plants thrive in bright light with a little shade.

## 104    ONCIDIUM FIMBRIATUM Lindl.
(Cymbidieae, Oncidiinae)

**Origin** Brazil.
**Description** Medium-sized plant. The pseudobulbs are fusiform, about 4 in (10 cm) tall, closely grouped on the rhizome, with fine longitudinal grooves that appear with age; the 2 apical leaves are lanceolate, suberect, coriaceous but flexible, about 6 in (15 cm) long and about 2 in (5 cm) wide. The inflorescence is basal, curved, stiff, dense and branched 16–20 in (40–50 cm) long. The yellow flowers with red-brown spots measure about 1 in (2 cm) across, are long-lasting and open all together. The orchid flowers in spring.
**Cultivation** This species, although not very commonly col-lected, is easy to grow and lavish with its flowers. It is best to raise it in small pots and to use finely chopped bark as a grow-ing medium. Watering should be regular all year round, slightly reduced after complete vegetational growth. Repotting can be done every other year.

## 105 ONCIDIUM GARDNERI Lindl.
(Cymbidieae, Oncidiinae)

**Synonym** *Oncidium flabelliferum* Paxt.
**Origin** Brazil.
**Description** Medium-sized plant. The pseudobulbs, 2–3 in (5–7 cm) tall, are ovoid, much compressed, longitudinally grooved with age, and grouped closely on the rhizome. The leaves, 2 per pseudobulb, are apical, oblong-lanceolate, coriaceous but flexible, 6–12 in (15–30 cm) long and 1–2 in (3–5 cm) wide. The inflorescence is basal, stiff, curved, branched and lax, composed of many flowers, and measuring almost 3 ft (1 m) in length. The largish, long-lasting flowers, which are yellow, with a fairly plentiful sprinkling of brown spots, measure about 2 in (5 cm) across. The orchid flowers in summer.
**Cultivation** This species, like the related *O. forbesii* Hooker, *O. marshallianum* Rchb. f. and *O. crispum* Lodd., is best grown in medium-small pots. The recommended medium is finely chopped bark. Regular watering throughout the year needs to be reduced after completion of the new growth.

## 106 ONCIDIUM LURIDUM Lindl.
(Cymbidieae, Oncidiinae)

**Synonym** *Oncidium guttatum* Rchb. f.
**Origin** Central America, West Indies, Florida, northern part of South America.
**Description** Medium-large plant, without pseudobulbs. The leaves, 8–20 in (20–50 cm) long, are oblong-oval (a shape commonly described as "mule eared"), erect, stiff, fleshy, and closely grouped on the rhizome. The inflorescence is stiff, curved, branched and lax, generally over 5 ft (1.5 m) in length. The conspicuous, long-lasting flowers are very variable in color, measure 1½ in (3–4 cm) across and open simultaneously. This species is sometimes confused with the similar *O. carthagenense* (Jacq.) Sw., but differs from the latter in that the central lobe of the lip is broader than the lateral lobes.
**Cultivation** An easily grown plant that needs to be kept in a pot proportional to its size. The recommended growing medium is bark, but osmunda fiber or other material can also be used provided there is good drainage. Watering should be regular all year round; but the compost should be allowed to dry out almost completely between applications, especially after flowering and before the plant throws out new growth.

## 107 ONCIDIUM MACROPETALUM Lindl.
(Cymbidieae, Oncidiinae)

**Origin** Bolivia, Brazil, Paraguay.
**Description** Small plant with conical-ovoid, angular pseudobulbs, 1 in (2–3 cm) tall, grouped close together, with 2 apical leaves that are coriaceous yet flexible, linear-lanceolate, curved and lax, about 4 in (10 cm) long. The basal, curved, lax inflorescence, about 8 in (20 cm) long, consists of a few long-lasting flowers, which are bright yellow with purple blotching, fairly big in relation to the size of the plant – 1 in (2–3 cm) in diameter. The orchid flowers in winter.
**Cultivation** This species may be grown either in a small pot with finely chopped bark or on a tree-fern raft. Raft specimens need more attention, particularly during the growth period; in fact, the compost should never be allowed to dry out entirely. Repotting should be carried out only when the medium, in the course of breaking up, retains too much water.

## 108 ONCIDIUM ONUSTUM Lindl.
(Cymbidieae, Oncidiinae)

**Origin** Colombia, Ecuador, Panama, Peru.
**Description** Medium-small plant. The pseudobulbs, 1 in (2–3 cm) tall, are conical-ovoid, longitudinally grooved, close together, and a gray-green with purple spots. The single apical leaf is erect, very coriaceous, about 4 in (10 cm) long. The basal, curved, fairly lax inflorescence varies in length and number of flowers according to the vigor of the plant. The long-lasting flowers are completely yellow and measure 1 in (2 cm) across. The orchid normally flowers in autumn.
**Cultivation** This species should be grown on a tree-fern raft or on cork. Regular watering during the growing period should be almost completely suspended later until new growth appears. It is a difficult species to handle; once removed from the substratum, it does not always root with sufficient vigor. It requires fairly bright light with a little shade.

## 109 ONCIDIUM ORNITHORHYNCHUM Kunth
(Cymbidieae, Oncidiinae)

**Origin** Costa Rica, Guatemala, El Salvador, Mexico.
**Description** Medium-sized plant. The pseudobulbs are oval, compressed, fairly closely grouped, about 2½ in (6 cm) tall. As a rule there are 2 apical leaves, flexible, curved, linear-lanceolate, about 8 in (20 cm) long. The inflorescences, sometimes 2 per pseudobulb, are basal, curving or pendulous, dense and branched, made up of numerous long-lasting pink flowers, about 1 in (2 cm) in diameter. The orchid flowers in winter.
**Cultivation** An easily grown plant, very widely collected. It is best cultivated in medium-small pots with finely chopped bark. Well-tended plants increase quickly. The species may be kept in the coolest part of the temperate greenhouse or even in a coolhouse; in the latter case watering should not be excessive since this is likely to encourage bacterial or fungal disease. Repotting and division are best done only when the compost begins to disintegrate.

## 110 ONCIDIUM PULCHELLUM Hook.
(Cymbidieae, Oncidiinae)

**Origin** West Indies.
**Description** Medium-small plant, without pseudobulbs. The dozen or so leaves, arranged fanwise, are stiff, coriaceous, linear-lanceolate, carinate, about 4 in (10 cm) long, often with finely dentate margins. The stiff, upright, sometimes branched flower stem bears a variable number of flowers (10–20) measuring about 1 in (2 cm) across. These are pale pink, long-lasting and open in swift succession. The orchid normally flowers in summer.
**Cultivation** This species is generally grown on a tree-fern raft or on cork, or sometimes even in a small pot. In the former case, it needs to be sprayed frequently with water so that the substratum does not dry out, because the thin roots cannot stand prolonged drought. In the latter case care has to be taken that the medium does not become waterlogged.
**Hybrids** In the last 15 years or so the species that belong to the group of so called equitant oncidiums have been widely used for hybridization, producing particularly beautiful and colorful clones. Species most frequently used for this purpose are: *O. compressicaule, O. guianense, O. pulchellum, O. pusillum, O. triquetrum, O. urophyllum* and *O. variegatum*.

Left: *Oncidium pulchellum*
Right: *O. Misty Pink × O. pulchellum*.

## 111 ONCIDIUM SPHACELATUM Lindl.
(Cymbidieae, Oncidiinae)

**Synonym** *Oncidium massangei* C. Morr.
**Origin** El Salvador, Guatemala, Honduras, Mexico.
**Description** Large plant with light, yellowish-green leaves. The pseudobulbs, about 4 in (10 cm) tall, are ovoid, strongly compressed, and set well apart on the rhizome. The 2–3 apical, linear leaves are erect, coriaceous yet flexible, up to 24 in (60 cm) long and about 1 in (3 cm) wide. The inflorescence, generally one per pseudobulb, erect or curved, dense and branched, may easily measure more than 3 ft (1 m) long in well-developed plants. The yellow and brown flowers, about ¾ in (2 cm) across, are long-lasting and open in quick succession. The orchid normally flowers in spring.
**Cultivation** *O. sphacelatum* is easy to grow and is widely cultivated. It grows freely, forming large specimens, and it may be raised either in a pot or in a basket with any type of potting mix. Watering should ensure that the growing medium is kept moist but is not soaked, since this is likely to damage newly forming vegetation.

## 112 ONCIDIUM VARICOSUM Lindl.
(Cymbidieae, Oncidiinae)

**Origin** Brazil.
**Description** Medium-sized plant. The pseudobulbs, 2½–4 in (6–10 cm) tall, are ovoid, elongate, slightly compressed, and rugose. The 2–3 apical leaves are lanceolate, coriaceous but flexible, curved, about 8 in (20 cm) long and about 1½ in (3.5 cm) wide. The basal inflorescence, stiff, erect or curved, branched, lax, 20–40 in (50–100 cm) long, bears numerous flowers with a yellow, trilobed lip, the central lobe being very big and showy. The variety *rogersii* Rchb. f. is larger,with the central lobe about 2 in (5 cm) in diameter. The orchid flowers in autumn and winter.
**Cultivation** This species is grown in medium-small pots in finely chopped bark. After new growth is complete, watering should be sufficient to keep the compost moist between successive applications; the species is easily damaged by a medium that is too wet and needs a slightly higher temperature than that given to many others of the same genus. Occasionally it forms well-grown specimens if left undisturbed.

## 113 OPHRYS BOMBYLIFLORA Link
(Orchideae, Orchidinae)

**Origin** Fairly well distributed in coastal regions of the Mediterranean, Canaries, Portugal.
**Description** Medium-small terrestrial plant, with 2 or more small, roundish underground tubers. The 4–6 fairly broad, short, elliptic-lanceolate leaves are arranged in a basal rosette. The erect, lax inflorescence is made up of 1–5 flowers and is long in relation to their number. The green and brown flowers are about 1 in (2 cm) in diameter and open in slow succession. The lip is trilobed with an abundance of hairs on the lateral lobes and at the tip of the central lobe. The orchid flowers in spring. This species is sometimes found on poor scrubland and arid pastures.

The genus flourishes in most parts of Europe, in western Asia and in Africa north of the Sahara. Some of the more than 50 species are quite rare and localized, and need careful and strict protection: however, the Berne Convention prohibits commerce in all wild European orchids, as in certain exotic species.

## 114 ORCHIS MILITARIS L.
(Orchideae, Orchidinae)

**Origin** Central and southern Europe, British Isles.
**Description** Medium-sized terrestrial plant furnished with 2 small, ovoid underground tubers. The 7–10 leaves are broadly lanceolate, glossy, fairly close together on the stem, the upper ones forming a sheath. The upright stem, 8–20 in (20–50 cm) long, bears a fairly dense inflorescence which gets longer as it blooms and is made up of numerous white and purple flowers. The sepals and petals are arranged in clusters and the divided central lobe of the trilobed lip is especially big and provided with a spur. The orchid flowers from mid to late spring. This species is to be found in wet or dry hill pastures and lowlands, depending on latitude, and in open woodland. *Orchis* species are protected in some countries as constituents of the wild flora.

## 115 ORNITHOCEPHALUS INFLEXUS Lindl.
(Maxillarieae, Ornithocephalinae)

**Synonym** *Ornithocephalus elaphas* Rchb. f.
**Origin** Costa Rica, Guatemala, Honduras, Mexico.
**Description** Small plant without pseudobulbs and with a very short stem. The leaves are linear, pointed, imbricate, arranged fanwise, stiff, fleshy, 1½–4 in (4–10 cm) long and about ¼ in (0.5 cm) wide. The axillary inflorescence, about as long as the leaf, is usually composed of many small green-white flowers that open in swift succession. The orchid flowers in winter.
**Cultivation** The *Ornithocephalus* orchids, as a rule, are delicate plants to be grown by experts. This species is best grown on a tree-fern raft or on cork, and because the slender, fragile roots require constant moisture, the base of the plant should be covered with a little sphagnum. Watering should be regular throughout the year. On hot summer days the plants benefit from frequent spraying with water. Well-tended specimens grow quite freely and produce several inflorescences at the same time.

---

## 116 PABSTIA JUGOSA (Lindl.) Garay
(Maxillarieae, Zygopetalinae)

**Synonyms** *Colax jugosus* (Lindl.) Lindl., *Maxillaria jugosa* Lindl.
**Origin** Brazil.
**Description** Medium-sized plant. The pseudobulbs are elongate-ovoid, slightly compressed, longitudinally grooved, about 2½ in (6 cm) tall, with 2 leaves at the apex. The leaves are lanceolate, coriaceous but flexible, plicate, 6–10 in (15–25 cm) long and about 1½ in (4 cm) wide. The basal flower stems, usually erect, about 6 in (15 cm) high, bear 2–4 large, slightly campanulate, white and purple flowers that are long-lasting and very showy. The orchid flowers in late spring and early summer.
**Cultivation** This species, one of the 4–5 that belong to the genus, is not very difficult to grow and produces quite beautiful flowers; nevertheless it is not widely cultivated. The plant should be grown in medium-sized, well-drained pots. The most suitable medium is bark. Watering should be regular all year round, but slightly reduced after full growth of the new vegetation. Repotting and division need be done only when the plants are well developed.

## 117 PAPHIOPEDILUM Pfitz.
(Cypripedioideae)

**Origin** Southeastern China, Philippines, India, Indonesia, New Guinea and adjacent islands, Indochinese peninsula.

**Description** Large, medium and medium-small plants, mostly terrestrial, without pseudobulbs. The rhizome, in the majority of species, is very short, so that vegetational parts are quite close together, but in certain species, such as *P. armeniacum* S.C. Chen & Liu and *P. druryi* (Bedd.) Stein, it is elongated and the growths are several inches apart. The leaves, varying in numbers per shoot according to species, are generally fairly coriaceous and are variable in shape, size and coloration. In many species they are linear, as, for example, in *P. insigne* (Wall. ex Lindl.) Pfitz., *P. villosum* (Lindl.) Stein and *P. philippinense* (Rchb. f.) Stein, whereas in others they are elliptic-oblong, as in *P. sukhakulii* Schoser et Senghas, *P. callosum* (Rchb. f.) Stein and *P. concolor* (Lindl.) Pfitz. In the majority of cases they are of average length; sometimes, as in *P. rothschildianum* (Rchb. f.) Stein, they measure more than 3 ft (1 m) long. The upper side in many species is uniformly green, but in a number of others it is fairly prominently spotted or tesselated, as in the subgenus *Brachypetalum* although even in this group there are exceptions: in *P. emersonii* Koopwitz & Cribb it is uniformly green. Often the lower side may display violet-brown patches and spots, which are quite widely distributed, as in *P. charlesworthii* (Rolfe) Pfitz., *P. malipoense* Chen & Tsi and *P. victoriaregina* (Sander) M. Wood; in *P. venustum* (Wall.) Pfitz. ex Stein this coloration covers such a broad area as to give the impression of gray-green marbling. In *P. liemianum* (Fowlie) Karasawa & Saito the leaf margin has short, slender hairs. The inflorescence is apical, stiff, generally erect or curved, varied in length, pubescent or not, and bears 1–2 or numerous flowers that open in succession; in *P. bellatulum* (Rchb. f.) Stein and *P. godefroyae* (Godefroy-Lebeuf) Stein, for example, the inflorescence is so short that often the flower rests on the leaf itself, while in the majority of other species it is 8–12 in (20–30 cm) long, bearing a great number of flowers. Very vigorous specimens of species that generally have a single flower per stem may produce two, this characteristic being the norm in certain species like *P. niveum* (Rchb. f.) Stein and *P. delenatii* Guill; the inflorescences of other species, such as *P. rothschildianum*, *P. parishii* (Rchb. f.) Stein, etc., are made up of 5–6 or more flowers, and *P. victoriaregina* may produce up to 33 but in this species only 1–2 are open at any one time. The flowers very conspicuous and long-lasting, vary in color, pattern, size and shape, even within the same species. There are species with flowers that measure only a couple of inches in diameter, (*P. concolor* for example) or more than 8 in (20 cm) (*P. rothschildianum*). *P. sanderianum* (Rchb. f.) has pendulous, spiraling petals that may be as much as 3 ft (1 m) or so in length. The form of the lip, characteristically sac-like, varies from species to species

Above left: *Paphiopedilum villosum* (Lindl.) Stein
Above right: *Paphiopedilum philippinense* (Rchb. f.) Stein
Below left: *Paphiopedilum concolor* (Lindl.) Pfitz.
Below right: *Paphiopedilum insigne* (Wall. ex Lindl.). Pfitz.

and there may be, within a single genus, four fundamental types. The period of flowering depends on the species in question but it usually occurs once a year.

**Cultivation** Not all the 60 or so species belonging to this genus are equally widespread in collections. Some are extremely rare, whereas others are very common and include a few that adapt to localized areas and far from ideal conditions. The *Paphiopedilum* orchids are generally grown in fairly small pots, often deeper than they are wide, because the root system, although not particularly extensive, tends to go deep down. Today, especially in the case of complex hybrids, which are less demanding, many types of potting media may be used: bark, sphagnum, osmunda fiber, perlite, charcoal, loam, volcanic lava or fiberglass and often a mixture of several of these elements is preferred. However, the most popular and perhaps the most recommended growing media, particularly for many botanical species, are osmunda fiber or finely chopped bark mixed with sphagnum. Some species, such as *P. parishii* and *P. lowii* (Lindl.) Stein, can also be grown on cork with sphagnum arranged around the roots, but such plants require special attention because the substratum must never be allowed to dry out. For pot-grown plants watering should be reasonably frequent throughout the year, depending on the surrounding conditions. Make sure that the medium is always kept moist but take care that there is no standing water, especially in the leaf axils, since this may cause rotting, to which these plants are liable. As a rule, to obtain plenty of flowers, complex hybrids should be fed regularly with doses half the concentration of those given to most other orchids, no matter which medium is used. This also applies to the multiflowered species and those with green and marbled leaves. Those of the *Brachypetalum* group, on the other hand, are best left unfed and grown in bark and sphagnum. Good results may also be obtained by growing these plants in leafmold, with or without sphagnum. In this case it is best not to administer any fertilizer. As regards temperature, very broadly speaking, both the *Paphiopedilum* hybrids and species are plants for the temperate greenhouse. But distinctions have to be made in some cases. For instance, the Indian species, such as *P. insigne, P. druryi, P. spicerianum* (Rchb. f. ex Masters et T. Moore) Pfitz., *P. fairrieanum* (Lindl.) Stein, etc., need a higher temperature both by day and night, and during the summer a daytime temperature of about 86°F (30°C) or above is recommended. Yet other species, like *P. rothschildianum,* although normally kept at temperatures that are not too cool, need a nighttime temperature of 53°F (12°C) during the 2–3 month rest period in order to flower properly. A humidity factor that is constantly above 60 percent, fairly shady surroundings and good ventilation are other indispensable conditions for the successful cultivation of *Paphiopedilum* orchids. It is advisable to repot both complex hybrids and species every three years, and it is a good idea to divide only well-developed plants so as to obtain specimens of at least three growths, (however, some species, especially those of the subgenus *Brachypetalum*, object to this procedure and are best left undivided). The *Paphiopedilum* orchids are not as a rule prone

Right: *Paphiopedilum micranthum* Tang & Wang

to attacks by parasites, and when necessary these can be controlled by spraying with insecticides or acaricides. But they are subject to fungal and bacterial diseases, perhaps stimulated by the constantly moist growing medium. Such diseases can be prevented by spraying regularly every 2–3 months with fungicides.

**Hybrids** The *Paphiopedilum* orchids are certainly one of the most popular genera, both as cut flowers (basically complex hybrids) and as collectors' plants, thanks largely, to hybridization. In form, color, tonality, pattern and duration, the hybrids of this genus are on a par with many others. Every year specialists and enthusiasts register hundreds of new hybrids that have been obtained either by intercrossing complex hybrids or by crossing these with wild species. The results are often extremely interesting. The first *Paphiopedilum* hybrid was introduced at the Chelsea Show of 1869 by the firm of Veitch and was a cross between *P. villosum* and *P. barbatum* (*P.* Harrisianum). It is hard to draw up a list of those species most used in hybridization, because almost all have been involved; and of all the many famous hybrids that have originated valuable clones, the following deserve special

Below: *Paphiopedilum haynaldianum* (Rchb. f.) Stein
Opposite above: *Paphiopedilum callosum* (Rchb. f.) Stein
Opposite below: *Paphiopedilum hirsutissimum* (Lindl. ex Hook.) Stein

mention: Winston Churchill, Hellas, Orchilla, Chianti, Betty Bracey, Milmoore, Sandra Mary, Pacific Ocean, Grand Canyon, Chardmoore, Yerba Buena, Inca, Paeony, F.C. Puddle, Miller's Daughter, Dusty Miller, Rosie Dawn, Solferino, Rosewood, Mildred Hunter, Sparsholt, etc. Some of these hybrids, as well as others not listed here, have produced other excellent hybrids.

Below: *Paphiopedilum sukhakulii* Schoser & Senghas × *P. Goultenianum*
Opposite above: *Paphiopedilum* Winston Churchill 'Indomitable' FCC/RHS
Opposite below: *Paphiopedilum* 'Westonbirt' FCC/RHS

## 118 PESCATOREA CERINA (Lindl.) Rchb. f.
(Maxillarieae, Zygopetalinae)

**Synonyms** *Huntleya cerina* Lindl., *Zygopetalum cerinum* (Lindl.) Rchb. f.
**Origin** Costa Rica, Panama.
**Description** Medium-sized plant without pseudobulbs. The leaves, generally 8 in number, are distichous, arranged fanwise, curved, membranous, linear-lanceolate, 8–24 in (20–60 cm) long and 1–2 in (3–5 cm) wide. The axillary flower stem, stiff, erect or curved, is 1½–4 in (4–10 cm) long and bears a single flower that measures about 2 in (5 cm) in diameter; it is white and greenish-yellow, long-lasting and very showy. The orchid flowers from spring to autumn.

**Cultivation** This species appreciates slightly lower temperatures than others of the same genus and therefore should be kept in the coolest part of the greenhouse. The *Pescatorea* orchids should be grown in a cool, moist and airy environment, with frequent watering throughout the year. Make sure that water is not left standing among the newly forming young leaves. If well cultivated, this plant develops freely and also produces several flowers.

---

## 119 PESCATOREA LEHMANNII Rchb. f.
(Maxillarieae, Zygopetalinae)

**Synonym** *Zygopetalum lehmannii* Rchb. f.
**Origin** Colombia, Ecuador.
**Description** Medium-sized plant without pseudobulbs. The leaves, generally 6–7 in number, linear-lanceolate, pointed, membranous, are arranged fanwise and measure 12–20 in (30–50 cm) long and about 2 in (4.5 cm) wide. The flower stem, always shorter than the leaves, is stiff, erect or curved, axillary and bears a single very showy, and long-lasting flower 2–2½ in (5–6 cm) in diameter. It is white with petals and sepals variously flushed with purple; the central lobe of the lip is densely covered with papillae. The orchid may flower several times a year, generally in spring.

**Cultivation** This species is usually grown in medium-small, well-drained pots. The medium can be either osmunda fiber or medium-chopped bark. Watering should keep the compost constantly moist but not waterlogged. It is best to repot only when necessary, particularly in the case of well-developed specimens, since these plants do not like to be disturbed.

## 120 **PHALAENOPSIS** Blume
(Vandeae, Sarcanthinae)

**Origin** Northern Australia, Philippines, India, Indonesia, Indochinese peninsula.

**Description** Small, medium and large plants without pseudobulbs, monopodial in structure. The stem, usually very small and sheathed by the base of the leaves, puts out thick roots. The leaves, generally 4–5 in number, are elliptic, obovate or lanceolate, alternate, fleshy, grouped close together, and of variable size and color according to species: in *P. gigantea* J.J. Smith, for example, the leaves may be about 3 ft (1 m) long, in *P. parishii* Rchb. f. 4–6 in (10–15 cm); in *P. stuartiana* Rchb. f. and *P. schilleriana* Rchb. f. they are very dark green with purple and silver-gray marbling, in *P. lueddemanniana* Rchb. f. and *P. mannii* Rchb. f. very bright green. The flower stems, axillary, stiff, fairly long, branched or simple, erect, horizontal or pendulous, bear only a few flowers, as in *P. amboinensis* J.J. Smith, or a large number, as in *P. stuartiana;* furthermore in certain species, such as *P. cornu-cervi* (Breda) Bl. et Rchb. f. and *P. violacea* Witte, flowers may be produced for several successive years on the same inflorescence. The flowers, which open one after another, vary considerably in size, consistency, shape, color, tonality and pattern, even within the same species. The flowering period varies according to species and often continues for several months, given that the flowers are very long-lasting.

**Cultivation** The 50 or so species that belong to the genus *Phalaenopsis* and the many thousands of hybrids all have similar cultural needs. As a rule they are grown in small, medium or large pots to suit not only the height of the plants but also, and more importantly, to accommodate the root mass; a pot that is too big is likely to impede healthy and well-branched root development, and a medium that is not penetrated by the roots tends to trap too much moisture, with serious consequences for the plants. Certain species, like *P. parishii*, are best grown on cork or on a tree-fern raft; others, such as *P. gigantea*, can equally well be grown in hanging baskets. The growing medium generally used nowadays for these plants is medium-chopped bark, but osmunda fiber, perlite and fiberglass are also suitable. The *Phalaenopsis* species are described as hothouse orchid plants that have an optimum temperature of between 62–64°F (17–18°C) and 80–82°F (27–28°C). These temperature limits must be considered in conjunction with other parameters which are extremely important for the health of the plants: humidity, light, watering, feeding and ventilation. During winter, temperatures of 62°F (17°C) at night and 71°F (22°C) by day, a humidity factor of 70 percent or above, and good ventilation constitute optimum conditions. The shading for the glass should also be reduced. By contrast, in summer, when the main problems are high temperature and too much light, you must provide plenty of shade, moisture and

Above left: *Phalaenopsis violacea* (Malaysian form)
Above right: *Phalaenopsis violacea* (Borneo form)
Below left: *Phalaenopsis lueddemanniana*
Below right: *Phalaenopsis schilleriana*

ventilation. A simple but effective method of judging whether *Phalaenopsis* orchids are being grown under correctly balanced conditions is to keep a constant watch all year round on their leaf color and flower production. In the modern hybrids the color of the leaves should be grass-green, neither too dark (tending to bottle-green) through lack of light, nor too pale (tending to yellow) as a result of excessive light. The production throughout the year of at least two inflorescences in an adult plant is a sign of good health and a properly balanced cultivation technique. Scarcity of light leads to feeble plants that are prone to attack by parasites of all kinds and that produce few flowers. Too much light, on the other hand, may result in dangerous and ugly scorching of the leaves. If, in addition, there is too little moisture in the surrounding air and the growing medium, growth will be stunted, there will be few if any flowers, and in extreme cases the plants may die. *Phalaenopsis* orchids should be watered regularly throughout the year, on average once a week but if necessary a few days early or late according to the surroundings and the growing medium being used. Small plants kept in small pots need to be watered more often than big ones. Adult plants should be repotted every three years and young plants every year. The best time to do this is between April and August, depending on the condition of the vegetation; a plant that has started to produce new roots and that will eventually have flower stems of not more than a few inches

Below: *Phalaenopsis parishii*
Opposite above: *Phalaenopsis amboinensis*
Opposite below: *Phalaenopsis stuartiana*

is in an ideal state for repotting. The roots must be freed from the old compost and those showing signs of rotting or scorching as a result of too much fertilizer should be removed; the portion of the stem that remains in the pot and any roots that are too long and are growing out of the pot should be shortened; and at this stage great care should be taken not to damage the new roots. The potting mix, moist but not sodden, must be sprinkled between the roots and lightly pressed down; it should come up to the neck of the plants, an inch or so beneath the lowest leaf. After being repotted, the plant should be handled normally.

**Hybrids** The *Phalaenopsis* orchids constitute one of the groups most widely used for hybridization, and of the thousands of clones thus obtained a very large number have commercial value, both as cut flowers and collectors' plants. The first white hybrid, which may justifiably be regarded as the founding parent of the principal lines of subsequent hybrids, was *P.* Elisabethae (*amabilis* × *rimestadiana*), registered by the firm of Vacherot Lecoufle in 1927. It is interesting to note that today, whereas *P. rimestadiana* is considered synonymous with *P. amabilis*, *P.* Elisabethae is no more than a particularly lovely clone of *P. amabilis*. This hybrid proved to be an extraordinary parent, direct and indirect, of hybrids which today are famous: Doris, Cast Iron Monarch, Palm Beach, Princess Grace, Ramona, Juanita, Hermosa, Polar Bear, Alice

Below: *Phalaenopsis* Redfan 'Grazia'.
Opposite above: *Phalaenopsis* 'La Storta' (*Phalaenopsis* Vallauris × *Phalaenopsis fuscata*).
Opposite below: *Phalaenopsis* Antonio Caruana 'Roma'.

Gloria, Keith Shaffer, Wilma Hughes, Henriette Lecoufle, Joseph Hampton, etc. The most outstanding white clones have also played a fundamental part in the search for flowers of other colors: thus the pink species *P. sanderiana* and *P. schilleriana* have originated Grand Coné, Versailles, Rêve Rose, Marmouset, Zada, Barbara Beard, Mistinguett, Best Girl, etc. Quite recently, too, efforts have intensified to obtain *Phalaenopsis* of many shades and tones, and unusual combinations of spots and streaks, using virtually all the wild species, crossing them both with one another and with hybrids of various colors. As a result we have red and orange flowers: George Vasquez, Princess Kaiulani, Fire Light, etc.; yellow and green flowers: Golden Sands, Golden Emperor, Bamboo Baby, etc.; flowers with horizontal or vertical streaks, and with large or small spots: Golden Pride, Spica, Deventeriana, Samba, George Moler, Marquise, Firedance, Frisson, Alida, Golden Amboin, Barbara Moler, etc; and a host of flowers, too many to mention, in single colors and flushed tones. The vast range of shapes and colors now available has made this genus of orchids one of the most popular of the entire family.

The genus is also used in crosses with species belonging to various other genera: *Doritis (Doritaenopsis), Vanda (Vandaenopsis), Ascocenda (Asconopsis), Aërides (Aëridopsis), Renanthera (Renanthopsis), Arachnis (Arachnopsis)* and *Vandopsis (Phalandopsis).*

Above: *Phalaenopsis* Estrella Rojo × George Vasquez
Below: *Phalaenopsis* Antarctic

## 121 PHOLIDOTA ARTICULATA Lindl.
(Coelogyneae, Coelogyninae)

**Synonym** *Pholidota decurva* Ridl.
**Origin** Java, Indochinese peninsula.
**Description** Medium-sized plant. The pseudobulbs are cylindrical, about 4 in (10 cm) tall, each new pseudobulb arising either from the apex or the base of the preceding pseudobulb, sometimes erect in habit, sometimes pendulous; they are often pinkish-green. The apical leaves, 2 per pseudobulb, are elliptic, coriaceous, about 4 in (10 cm) long and about 1 in (3 cm) wide. The inflorescence, apical, curved, about 6 in (15 cm) long, bears 10–16 flowers of about ½ in (1 cm), greenish or pinkish-white, campanulate and supported by a large deciduous bract. The orchid generally flowers in summer.
**Cultivation** A limited number of species are ascribed to this genus, none as a rule is widely found in collections. It is best to grow *P. articulata* in small pots, but it can also be grown on cork or on a branch. The recommended potting medium is finely chopped bark. Watering should be regular during new plant growth and markedly reduced later. Repotting should be done only when necessary; in fact, these plants do not like being disturbed.

---

## 122 PHRAGMIPEDIUM PEARCEI (Rchb. f.) Senghas & Rauh.
(Cypripedioideae)

**Synonym** *Selenipedium pearcei* Rchb. f.
**Origin** Colombia, Costa Rica, Ecuador, Panama.
**Description** Medium-large terrestrial plant without pseudobulbs. The growths are close together on the creeping rhizome. The leaves are distichous, coriaceous, linear, pointed, curved, 16–20 in (40–50 cm) long and 1–½ in (3–4 cm) wide. The apical flower stem is stiff, erect and pubescent, bearing a number of flowers, each one opening as soon as another fades. They are large and showy, long-lasting, with pendulous petals, folded slightly spirally, measuring over 4 in (10 cm). They are green, white and purple in color. The orchid flowers in summer.
**Cultivation** Grow in a pot proportional to the size of the plant in osmunda fiber or bark with an addition of sphagnum. Keep the compost moist, but take care not to overwater since this rots the roots. Feed every 15 days in half-doses. The plants should be repotted and divided only when well developed.
**Hybrids** Some species of *Phragmipedium* have been used for hybridization. Among the best known primary hybrids are: *P. Grande* (*caudatum* (Lindl.) Rolfe × *longifolium* (Warsc. et Rchb. f.) Rolfe), *P. Sedenii* (*schlimii* × *longifolium*), *P. Dominianum* (*caricinum* (Lindl. & Paxt.) Rolfe × *caudatum*) and *P. Schroderae* (*caudatum* × Sedenii).

## 123 PHRAGMIPEDIUM SCHLIMII (Linden & Rchb. f.)
Rolfe
(Cypripedioideae)

**Synonyms** *Cypripedium schlimii* (Linden & Rchb. f.) Batem., *Selenipedium schlimii* Linden et Rchb. f., *Paphiopedilum schlimii* (Linden & Reichb. f.) Stein.
**Origin** Colombia.
**Description** Medium-sized terrestrial plant without pseudobulbs. The leaves, linear, pointed, suberect, coriaceous, at least 12 in (30 cm) long and about 1 in (2 cm) wide, are arranged, usually 8 in number, in a rosette. The erect, pubescent flower stem, in varying shades of purple, grows longer during flowering. The white and pink flowers, covered in a soft, dense down, 1½–2 in (4–5 cm) across, open one at a time; there are usually 4–5, sometimes up to 10. The orchid may flower more than once a year, normally in spring.
**Cultivation** This species should be grown in small-medium pots, with compost that retains moisture without becoming waterlogged. It is less luxuriant than other plants of the genus and more prone to rot. Feeding should be done every 15 days with half-doses. Repot only when the compost starts to decompose.

## 124 PLECTRELMINTHUS CAUDATUS (Lindl.)
Summerh.
(Vandeae, Aerangidinae)

**Synonym** *Angraecum caudatum* Lindl.
**Origin** Tropical West Africa.
**Description** Medium-sized plant without pseudobulbs. The stem is erect, generally 4–8 in (10–20 cm) high, with numerous alternate leaves, 8–12 in (20–30 cm) long, imbricate, curved, linear, unequally bilobed at the apex, coriaceous but flexible. The axillary inflorescence, curved or pendulous, 12–16 in (30–40 cm) long, usually carries 5–9 green and white flowers, set well apart, very showy and long-lasting, with a slightly spiraled spur which is at least 6 in (15 cm) long. The orchid flowers in autumn.
**Cultivation** The species is not very common in collections and needs to be grown on a piece of wood with some tufts of sphagnum set among the large roots. Watering should be frequent and regular throughout the year. Keep in a well lighted position with some shade from the direct rays of the sun.

## 125 PLEIONE MACULATA (Lindl.) Lindl.
(Coelogyneae, Coelogyninae)

**Synonym** *Coelogynae maculata* Lindl.
**Origin** Burma, northern India from Sikkim to Assam, Thailand.
**Description** Medium-small plant. The pseudobulbs are almost conical, close together on the rhizome, rugose, spotted brown, about 1 in (3 cm) tall, with two apical leaves, elliptic-lanceolate, deciduous, membranous, about 8 in (20 cm) long and about 1 in (3 cm) wide. The basal, single-flowered inflorescence sprouts from pseudobulbs that have lost their leaves. The flowers are delicate, of variable color, (but basically white and purple) and measure about 2½ in (6 cm) in diameter. The orchid flowers in autumn.

**Cultivation** This species, like others belonging to the same genus, should be grown in small pots. The ideal growing medium is a mixture of equal parts of sphagnum, osmunda fiber and finely chopped bark. During the growth period the plants need abundant watering and temperatures equivalent to those of the temperate greenhouse; after leaf drop a rest period at a lower temperature is necessary until the flower stems appear. Repotting should be done every year before flowering.

---

## 126 PLEUROTHALLIS PTEROPHORA Cogn.
(Epidendreae, Pleurothallidinae)

**Origin** Brazil.
**Description** Small plant without pseudobulbs. The slender, erect stems, very close together on the much-branched rhizome, several inches in length, bear an apical leaf, elliptic-obovate, coriaceous, suberect, spotted brown underneath, about 1½ in (6 cm) long and about 1 in (2 cm) wide. The stiff, erect axillary inflorescence, about 4 in (10 cm) long, is composed of many small, delicate white flowers that open simultaneously. The orchid may flower several times a year at different periods.

**Cultivation** More than 900 species are ascribed to this genus; all are from tropical America. The majority come from cool, wet, high mountain regions; others from hotter zones. It is best to grow these species in small pots with potting medium consisting of osmunda or finely chopped bark mixed with sphagnum. Both the compost and the surroundings should always be moist. Repotting should be done only when plants are well developed.

## 127 POLYSTACHYA AFFINIS Lindl.
(Polystachyeae)

**Origin** Tropical Africa.

**Description** Medium-small plant. The pseudobulbs, 1–2 in (2–5 cm) in diameter, are round, very compressed, and tightly attached to the substratum. There are normally 1–2 apical leaves, stalked, oblanceolate or elliptic, coriaceous but flexible, 4–10 in (10–25 cm) long and 1–1½ in (3–6 cm) wide. The apical inflorescence, erect or curved, rarely branched, lax, 8–12 in (20–30 cm) long is composed of many inconspicuous, long-lasting flowers that measure about ½ in (1 cm) across, their color ranging from white to yellow-green. The flower stem and the flowers themselves are pubescent. The orchid blooms in spring and summer.

**Cultivation** The 150 or so species belonging to the genus *Polystachya,* with a pantropical distribution, are quite commonly cultivated. This species can be grown on cork or on a tree branch with a little sphagnum arranged around the roots. It is easily cultivated and once properly attached to the substratum grows luxuriantly and flowers plentifully. Watering should be frequent during the growth period and slightly reduced thereafter.

## 128 POLYSTACHYA BELLA Summerh.
(Polystachyeae)

**Origin** Kenya.

**Description** Medium-small plant. The pseudobulbs are more or less oval, compressed, tightly packed together on a branched rhizome, several inches tall. The apical leaves, 1–2 per pseudobulb, coriaceous but flexible, suberect, are narrowly elliptic, 2½–5 in (6–12 cm) long and ½–1 in (1–2 cm) wide. The apical, sometimes branched flower stem, about 4 in (10 cm) long, bears many flowers that are characteristically longer than they are wide, yellow-orange with a red stripe on the tip opening in succession and of long duration. The orchid flowers in winter.

**Cultivation** This species is best grown on a tree branch or on cork with sphagnum around the roots. It is quite sturdy and flowers easily. Watering should be regular and plentiful during the growth period and subsequently reduced so that the substratum dries out between successive applications. Many *Polystachya* species deserve to be more widely cultivated because they are simple to grow and produce abundant flowers.

## 129 PROMENAEA XANTHINA (Lindl.) Lindl.
(Maxillarieae, Zygopetalinae)

**Synonyms** *Maxillaria xanthina* Lindl., *Promenaea citrina* D. Don.

**Origin** Brazil.

**Description** Small plant with tightly packed pseudobulbs, oval, compressed, with 4 corners, about 1 in (2 cm) tall. There are generally 2 apical, oblanceolate leaves, about 3 in (7 cm) long. The basal inflorescences, about 4 in (10 cm) long, bear 1–2 conspicuous, long-lasting, yellow flowers. The orchid flowers in summer.

**Cultivation** An easily grown plant that can form good specimens. It is advisable to raise it in shallow pots or baskets with a light, well-drained medium which is always moist during the growth stages. After that the plant should be given several weeks of rest. Take care when watering not to leave any water on the newly forming shoots, since these are prone to rotting.

## 130 RENANTHERA IMSCHOOTIANA Rolfe
(Vandeae, Sarcanthinae)

**Origin** Burma, northwest India, Vietnam.

**Description** Medium-sized plant without pseudobulbs. The erect stem, which becomes woody with age, rarely measuring more than 28 in (70 cm) in length and ¼ in (0.5 cm) in diameter, may throw out aerial roots. The many leaves are alternate, coriaceous, oblong and bilobed, usually under 4 in (10 cm) long and less than 1 in (2 cm) wide. The axillary inflorescences, stiff, horizontal, branched and lax, carry numerous very showy and long-lasting, red and yellow flowers, 1½ in (3–4 cm) across. The orchid usually flowers in early summer.

**Cultivation** These plants are grown in medium-small, well-drained pots. The medium generally consists of good-sized pieces of bark. They are easy to cultivate but need a very well-lighted position in order to flower; this should be slightly shaded in summer and in full sun in winter. Temperatures need to be cooler than those given to other species of the genus. Watering should be regular all year round.

## 131 RENANTHERA MONACHICA Ames
(Vandeae, Sarcanthinae)

**Origin** Philippines.
**Description** Medium-sized plant without pseudobulbs. The erect stem is 8–12 in (20–30 cm) high. The leaves are alternate, stiff, elliptic-linear, with an unequally bilobed apex, very dark green tinged purple-brown, about 4 in (10 cm) long. The axillary inflorescence, stiff, suberect and branched, 8–12 in (20–30 cm) long, bears many very long-lasting, conspicuous flowers, about 1 in (3 cm) in diameter, which are yellow, spotted with red, and open in rapid succession. The orchid flowers in spring.

**Cultivation** An easily grown plant that is best raised in medium-small pots, with well-drained medium. It is advisable to use bark although excellent results may be obtained with other growing media. Repotting should be carried out only when the potting mix shows signs of breaking up.
**Hybrids** Some species of this genus have been widely used to hybridize species of related genera such as: *Vanda (Renantanda), Phalaenopsis (Renanthopsis), Arachnis (Aranthera),* etc.; many of these hybrids have very attractive flowers.

---

## 132 RESTREPIA ANTENNIFERA H.B.K.
(Epidendreae, Pleurothallidinae)

**Synonym** *Pleurothallis ospinae* R.E. Schultes.
**Origin** Colombia, Ecuador, Venezuela.
**Description** Small plant without pseudobulbs. The stems are erect, close together on the rhizome, covered with dry, black-spotted sheaths, about 4 in (10 cm) long and bearing an erect, coriaceous, ovate or elliptic leaf, about 2 in (5 cm) long and ¾ in (2 cm) wide, at their apex. The flower stem, slender, axillary, erect or pendulous, about ¾–1¼ in (2–3 cm) long, bears a single flower, quite large for the plant's size, and white-yellow in color densely scattered with brownish-purple spots. The petals are characteristically filiform. The orchid generally flowers in spring.
**Cultivation** This species can be grown on a raft of tree fern or in small pots with a compost of osmund fiber and finely chopped bark mixed with sphagnum. This plant prefers a quite cool, humid and airy environment. The growing medium should always be kept moist but never waterlogged, so during hotter periods it will benefit from regular spraying. If well tended, this species will develop freely and flower plentifully.

## 133 RHYNCHOLAELIA DIGBYANA (Lindl.) Schltr.
(Epidendreae, Laeliinae)

**Synonym** *Brassavola digbyana* Lindl.
**Origin** Guatemala, Honduras, Mexico.
**Description** Medium-sized plant. The pseudobulbs, about 6 in (15 cm) tall, are fairly elongate, compressed, quite close together on the rhizome, with a single axillary leaf, elliptic, erect, stiff, fleshy, about 8 in (20 cm) long and about 2 in (5 cm) wide. The entire plant is glaucous. The axillary, erect flower stem bears a single large, showy, greenish-white flower, long-lasting and very conspicuous, with a greatly enlarged lip, fringed at the margin. The orchid flowers in spring.
**Cultivation** This species, like the related *R. glauca* (Lindl.) Schltr., can be grown either on bark, on a tree-fern raft or in a pot proportional to its size, with medium-chopped bark. The plants grow freely, forming well-proportioned specimens: but in order to flower there must be numerous pseudobulbs. Watering should be abundant during the growth period and subsequently reduced. The species requires more light than the *Cattleyas* with which they are often hybridized.
**Hybrids** *R. digbyana* has been widely used for the hybridization of species and hybrids of the following genera: *Cattleya, Laelia, Sophronitis, Epidendrum, Broughtonia* and *Diacrium*, in the denomination of which it appears as a member of the genus *Brassavola*. The special characteristics which such hybrids derive from this species are the dimensions and fringing of the lip.

---

## 134 RHYNCHOSTYLIS GIGANTEA (Lindl.) Ridley
(Vandeae, Sarcanthinae)

**Synonym** *Saccolabium giganteum* Lindl.
**Origin** Indochinese peninsula.
**Description** Medium-small plant with monopodial habit. The stem is generally at least 6 in (15 cm) high and produces many very thick roots. The alternate leaves, set very close together, are linear, curved, very coriaceous, unequally bilobed, 6–12 in (15–30 cm) long and about 1 in (3 cm) wide, and their base sheathes the stem itself. The axillary inflorescence, dense and curving, 8–12 in (20–30 cm) long, is composed of very many flowers that measure 1 in (2–3 cm); they are very showy and long-lasting, colored white with a fair sprinkling of purple spots. The orchid flowers in autumn and winter.
**Cultivation** Easily grown plant that should be cultivated in hanging baskets in a well-lighted position, with a growing medium consisting of large slivers of bark, charcoal or crock. These plants do not like being repotted and therefore, when this proves necessary, the old basket with its tightly attached roots should be placed inside a bigger one. Watering should be constant throughout the year.
**Hybrids** The *Rhynchostylis* species are commonly crossed with other species belonging to the subtribe Sarcanthinae.

## 135 RODRIGUEZIA BRACTEATA (Vell.) Hoehne
(Cymbidieae, Oncidiinae)

**Origin** Brazil.

**Description** Medium-small plant. The pseudobulbs are small, ovoid, fairly compressed, about 1 in (2 cm) tall, partly enfolded by the basal leaves and with 1–2 apical leaves that are coriaceous, stiff, linear, narrow, pointed, curved, dark green, 4–6 in (10–15 cm) long. The basal inflorescence, stiff and pendulous, usually 4–6 in (10–15 cm) long, sometimes more, is made up of numerous long-lasting, simultaneously opening white flowers with a large lip, about 1 in (2 cm) long and equipped with a spur. The orchid generally flowers in spring and summer.

**Cultivation** This species, like the majority of the other 35 or so that belong to the genus, can be grown either on a tree-fern raft, on cork or in small pots; in the last instance the growing medium may be osmunda fiber or a mixture of finely chopped bark and sphagnum. Watering of pot specimens should always be carried out with great care; those on rafts or on cork must never be allowed to dry out. Repot only when absolutely necessary.

## 136 RODRIGUEZIELLA GOMEZOIDES (Barb. Rodr.) O. Ktze.
(Cymbidieae, Oncidiinae)

**Synonym** *Theodorea gomezoides* Barb. Rodr.

**Origin** Eastern Brazil.

**Description** Small plant. The pseudobulbs are ovoid, elongate, compressed, 1 in (2–3 cm) tall, with 2 apical leaves, linear-lanceolate, pointed, about 4 in (10 cm) long and about ½ in (1 cm) wide. The basal, pendulous, lax inflorescence, usually a little shorter than the leaves, is composed of some 10 rather small, inconspicuous, delicate flowers that are yellow-green with a white lip. The orchid flowers in spring.

**Cultivation** This species can be grown either on a tree-fern raft, on cork or in small pots with any kind of medium, preferably one made up of bark mixed with sphagnum. Raft and cork specimens should never be allowed to dry out entirely. Watering should be plentiful and frequent during the growth period, then reduced. These plants are rather delicate and may die suddenly if conditions are not as indicated.

## 137 ROSSIOGLOSSUM GRANDE (Lindl.) Garay & Kennedy
(Cymbidieae, Oncidiinae)

**Synonym** *Odontoglossum grande* Lindl.
**Origin** Guatemala, Mexico.
**Description** Medium-small plant. The pseudobulbs are ovoid, rather compressed, about 2 in (5 cm) tall, colored gray-green. The apical leaves, 1–3 per pseudobulb, are coriaceous, elliptic or lanceolate, generally curved, 4–16 in (10–40 cm) long and about 2 in (5 cm) wide. The basal, stiff, erect inflorescence, 8–12 in (20–30 cm) long, is usually composed of 4–5 large, very showy flowers in varying shades of yellow sprinkled with brown spots. The flowers open in succession and last a couple of weeks. The orchid flowers from autumn to spring.
**Cultivation** This species comes from mountain zones above 9,000 ft (2,700 m) and therefore needs a constantly cool, moist and airy environment. The plants should be grown in medium-small pots, with soft, moist and well-drained compost. The species is sensitive to excessive heat and to standing water, especially during new growth. If well tended, the plants develop freely.

## 138 SARCOCHILUS HARTMANNII F. Muell.
(Vandeae, Sarcanthinae)

**Synonym** *Sarcochilus rubicentrum* Fitzg.
**Origin** Eastern Australia.
**Description** Medium-small plant with pseudobulbs. The stem, rarely longer than 4 in (10 cm), is erect, with 6–8 leaves that are oblong-lanceolate, coriaceous, stiff, falcate, 4–7 in (10–18 cm) long and about ½ in (1.5 cm) wide. The axillary, erect, dense inflorescence, usually as long as the leaves, carries up to 15 very showy, long-lasting flowers, about ½ in (1 cm) in diameter, normally white with concentric crimson blotches on the parts around the column; occasionally the flowers may be entirely white or crimson. The orchid flowers from late winter to early spring.
**Cultivation** Because of its abundance of flowers and their appearance, as well as its easy cultivation, this species is often collected. It is usually grown in small pots, preferably in a medium of finely chopped bark, but sometimes it is grown on cork with tufts of sphagnum around the roots. Watering should be regular during the growth period and subsequently reduced. If well cared for, the plants develop freely, forming small clumps that produce a number of inflorescences at the same time.

## 139 SCHOMBURGKIA SUPERBIENS (Lindl.) Rolfe
(Epidendreae, Laeliinae)

**Synonyms** *Cattleya superbiens* (Lindl.) Beer, *Laelia superbiens* Lindl.
**Origin** Guatemala, Honduras, Mexico.
**Description** Large plant. The pseudobulbs are fusiform, set well apart on the rhizome, longitudinally grooved, at least 12 in (30 cm) long with 2 apical leaves. These are lanceolate, sub-erect, very coriaceous, 12–16 in (30–40 cm) long and 2½ in (6–7 cm) wide. The apical, stiff, erect flower stem, more than 3 ft (1 m) long, bears at its tip numerous flowers measuring about 4 in (10 cm) across, colored purple; the trilobed lip has 5–6 longitudinal lamellae. The orchid flowers in winter.
**Cultivation** The *Schomburgkia* species are very easy to grow. They are usually raised in pots proportional to their size but can also be cultivated on cork or a piece of tree-fern fiber. To stimulate flowering, it is essential to place the plants in very bright positions, watering them frequently during growth so that the medium is always moist. Later watering should be reduced sufficiently to allow the substratum to dry out between applications. Repotting and division should be done only when absolutely necessary.

## 140 SCUTICARIA HADWENII (Lindl.) Hooker
(Maxillarieae, Maxillariinae)

**Synonym** *Bifrenaria hadwenii* Lindl.
**Origin** Brazil, Guyana.
**Description** Medium-sized plant with drooping habit. The pseudobulbs are cylindrical, close together, about 2 in (5 cm) long and about ¼ in (0.5 cm) across. The leaves are single, mostly pendulous, cylindrical, grooved, very dark green, 8–16 in (20–40 cm) long. The inflorescence, generally single-flowered, sprouts from the base of the pseudobulb and is curved or pendulous, 4–8 in (5–10 cm) long. The flower is very showy, yellow with a variable number of brown and red spots, and long-lasting, 2½ in (6 cm) in diameter. The orchid flowers from spring to autumn.
**Cultivation** Because of the habit of this species, it is usually grown on a tree-fern raft or on cork, but can also be raised in a basket with a medium consisting of bark mixed with either osmunda fiber or sphagnum. During the growth period the plants need frequent watering; after the flower drops it is best to give them a rest period of at least 3 weeks. *S. hadwenii*, in order to grow well and bloom, needs plenty of light with a little protection from the direct rays of the sun.

## 141 SEDIREA JAPONICA (Rchb. f.) Garay & Sweet
(Vandeae, Sarcanthinae)

**Synonym** *Aerides japonicum* Rchb. f.
**Origin** Japan, Korea.
**Description** Medium-small plant of monopodial structure with a short stem, sheathed at the base by the leaves. The 5–6 leaves are 3–4 in (8–10 cm) long and about 1 in (2 cm) wide, linear, rather fleshy, with a rounded tip. The axillary inflorescence is curved, lax, longer than the leaves, and made up of numerous white or greenish flowers, with purple bars on the lip, ½–1 in (1–2 cm) in diameter, which open in succession. The adult plants branch freely and produce a number of inflorescences simultaneously. The orchid flowers in spring and summer.
**Cultivation** This species, the only one of the genus, may be grown on cork, on a tree-fern raft or in a small pot, in which case medium-chopped bark is recommended. Watering should be regular all through the year. While repotting it is advisable to divide tillered plants.

## 142 SOBRALIA MACRANTHA Lindl.
(Arethuseae, Sobraliinae)

**Origin** From Mexico to Costa Rica.
**Description** Large terrestrial plant without pseudobulbs. The stems are 6½ ft (2 m) or more tall, thin, stiff, erect, with leaves along their entire length, fairly close together on the rhizome. The leaves, set far apart, are lanceolate, pointed, coriaceous, with prominent veining, 6–10 in (15–25 cm) long and up to 3 in (7 cm) wide. The flowers, produced one at a time from an extremely short apical inflorescence, are big and showy, not long-lasting, fairly deep purple with a white throat to the lip. The orchid flowers from spring to early autumn.
**Cultivation** An easy plant to grow, usually cultivated in fairly large pots because the root system is extensive and grows rapidly. Any kind of soil can be used. Repotting and division can be effected when the plants are large. The *Sobralia* species can be grown outdoors in the garden in countries where the winter climate permits.

## 143 SOPHRONITELLA VIOLACEA (Lindl.) Schltr.
(Epidendreae, Laeliinae)

**Synonym** *Sophronitis violacea* Lindl.
**Origin** Eastern Brazil.
**Description** Small plant. The pseudobulbs are fusiform, close together on the rhizome, longitudinally grooved, 1 in (2–3 cm) long and about ¼ in (0.5 cm) wide. The apical leaves, one per pseudobulb, are coriaceous, linear, pointed, slightly curved or erect, 1½–3 in (4–7 cm) long and under ¼ in (0.5 cm) wide. The axillary, erect flower stem generally bears a single flower, occasionally 2. This is fairly deep purple, very showy and long-lasting, about 1 in (2 cm) in diameter. The orchid flowers in winter.
**Cultivation** This species, the only one of its genus, may be grown either on a tree-fern raft or in a small pot with a mixture of finely chopped bark and sphagnum. Although *S. violacea* thrives in a constantly moist environment, watering should not be overdone because of the risk of rot. Repotting should be carried out only when necessary and for large plants.

---

## 144 SOPHRONITIS COCCINEA (Lindl.) Rchb. f.
(Epidendreae, Laeliinae)

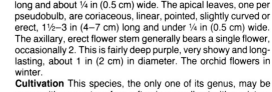

**Synonym** *Sophronitis grandiflora* Lindl.
**Origin** Eastern Brazil.
**Description** Small plant. The pseudobulbs are fusiform, very close together on the much branched rhizome, 1–1½ in (2–4 cm) long. The leaves, one per pseudobulb, are almost elliptic, erect, coriaceous, 1¼–2½ in (3–6 cm) long and about ½ in (1.5 cm) wide. The axillary flower stem, a few inches long, bears one flower that is fairly big for the size of the plant, very showy, generally scarlet. Yellow or pink-flowered specimens also occur and are much sought after. The orchid flowers in autumn and winter.
**Cultivation** Although this is a fairly commonly collected species, it is not easy to grow and it is rare to see luxuriant specimens. It may be grown either on a tree-fern raft or in a small pot with any type of medium provided it is well drained and always moist. This species cannot withstand periods of drought and therefore is likely to die quickly if not given regular watering. Other conditions indispensable for getting good results are a very well-lighted position and proper ventilation.
**Hybrids** This species, like the other 7 that belong to the same genus, has been widely used for hybridization with related genera such as *Cattleya, Laelia, Brassavola,* etc. The *Sophronitis* species generally produce descendants with orange-red coloration.

## 145 SPATHOGLOTTIS PLICATA Blume
(Arethuseae, Bletiinae)

**Synonyms** *Bletia angustata* Gagn., *Spathoglottis lilacina* Griff.

**Origin** Philippines, India, Indonesia, New Guinea, Indochinese peninsula.

**Description** Medium-sized terrestrial plant. The pseudobulbs are ovoid, about 3 in (7 cm) tall and about 2 in (5 cm) across. The numerous apical leaves are stalked, linear-lanceolate, pointed, plicate, membranous, sometimes more than 3 ft (1 m) long and 1–3 in (2–7 cm) wide. The terminal part of the stiff, erect flower stem, 8–12 in (20–30 cm) long but sometimes up to 3 ft (1 m), bears a fairly dense cluster of up to 25 showy purple or white flowers that open in succession. The orchid flowers several times a year.

**Cultivation** This species, like others of the same genus, is widely grown as a garden plant in various warm regions of the world; it needs a sunny position and light soil with plenty of organic matter. It can also be grown in a pot with a medium consisting of a mixture of osmunda fiber and sphagnum, with an adequate drainage layer. Whether in the open ground or in a pot, the pseudobulbs must always be above the surface. Watering should be frequent, especially during the new growth period.

## 146 SPIRANTHES L.C. Rich.
(Cranichideae, Spiranthinae)

**Origin** Temperate areas of both hemispheres.

**Description** Medium-small terrestrial plants with fibrous or tuberous roots. Approximately 300 species are ascribed to this somewhat polymorphous genus, although its precise character is still a source of systematic controversy. The leaves, variable in shape, are as a rule arranged in the form of a basal rosette; they are either persistent or caducous, present or absent during flowering, sometimes bractiform. The stiff, erect, fairly long inflorescence is composed of numerous tubular flowers that are quite small. These vary in color although they are usually greenish-white and arranged in a spiral. These plants grow freely in fields, meadows and savannas but are also found in woods and forests, both on acid and calcareous soil. They flower once a year, the period depending on the species and range. In Europe, *S. spiralis* (L.) Chevall. is the only orchid that blooms in the autumn.

Left: *Spiranthes cernua* (L.) L.C. Rich., North America.
Right: *Spiranthes spiralis* (L.) Chevall., Europe and Middle East.

## 147 STANHOPEA Hooker
(Cymbidieae, Stanhopeinae)

**Origin** Tropical areas from Mexico to Brazil.

**Description** Medium-large plants with a very short rhizome that produces a number of pseudobulbs. These are usually ovoid, packed tightly together, about 2 in (5 cm) tall, deeply furrowed, and bear a single leaf at the apex. The leaves, provided with a fairly long, grooved petiole, are broad, elliptic, plicate, coriaceous and glossy on the upper side, with prominent veining. The basal, drooping inflorescences consist of a variable number of flowers, generally large and very showy, in shades of cream, yellow and brown, highly scented but of short duration. The shape of the lip is characteristic of the genus: it is divided into three parts (hypochile, mesochile and epichile) which vary in size and shape according to the species, as is the case with the column. The orchids flower from late spring to early autumn.

**Cultivation** Although the flowers of *Stanhopea* orchids are short-lived, they are very popular with collectors. The plants are easy to cultivate, best grown in wide-mesh baskets that allow the inflorescences to snake out in all directions. A

Below: *Stanhopea insignis* Frost
Opposite: *Stanhopea oculata* (Lodd.) Lindl. (Synonyms: *S. bucephalus* Lindl., *S. guttata* Lindl.)

well-developed specimen produces several inflorescences almost simultaneously. The recommended growing media are sphagnum, osmunda or tree-fern fiber. Although repotting and division present no particular problems, the plants, in order to bloom abundantly, should ideally remain in their containers for several years, until the mix starts to deteriorate. The baskets should be hung in a well-lighted part of the greenhouse, with plenty of air and humidity. Stanhopeas are as a rule suited to the temperate greenhouse but can stand temperatures a good deal higher than those normally recommended – up to 95–104°F (35–40°C) – but at these levels, particularly with poor ventilation and low humidity, there is a risk of red spider mite infestation. Sunlight, unless screened, may cause leaf scorching. Watering should be plentiful during the growth period but subsequently reduced, if not stopped.

**Hybrids** Some *Stanhopea* species have been crossed with one another to produce very beautiful clones such as: *S.* Assidensis (*tigrina* × *wardii*), *S.* Mem. Paul Allen (*ecornuta* × *tigrina*), *S.* Bellaerensis (*insignis* × *oculata*), etc., but these are not widely available.

Below: *Stanhopea saccata* Batem. (Synonyms: *S. marshii* Rchb. f., *S. radiosa* Lem.)
Opposite above: *Stanhopea tigrina* Batem. (Synonym: *S. expansa* P.N. Don.)
Opposite below: *Stanhopea jenischiana* Kramer ex Rchb. f.

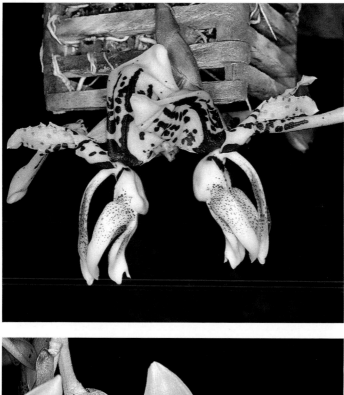

## 148 **STELIS** Sw.
(Epidendreae, Pleurothallidinae)

**Origin** Widespread in Central and South America.
**Description** Medium-small or small plants with pseudobulbs, with a thin, creeping, well-branched rhizome. The slender stems are stiff, erect, packed closely together on the rhizome so that in well-developed specimens they tend to form small clumps of growths. The single, apical leaves are coriaceous, suberect, stalked or sessile, variable in shape according to species but as a rule linear or elliptic-oblanceolate. The inflorescences, single or numerous, axillary, fairly long, are composed of many small or tiny flowers with connate sepals characteristically arranged in a triangle and very short petals and lip. In some species the green or brownish purple flowers open during the day and close at night, or visa versa. The orchids flower at different periods, depending on the species.
**Cultivation** These plants should be grown in small pots. The recommended medium is sphagnum, either on its own or mixed with osmunda fiber or finely chopped bark. Watering should be frequent so as to keep the mix always moist, for the roots of the plants must not be allowed to dry out. Shady, airy and moist surroundings are necessary because the small plants are rather delicate.

## 149 **THRIXSPERMUM FORMOSANUM** Schltr.
(Vandeae, Saracanthinae)

**Origin** Taiwan.
**Description** Small plant without pseudobulbs, monopodial in structure. The small stem is only a few inches long, sheathed by the base of the leaves which are alternate, linear, pointed, stiff, slightly fleshy, 2–3 in (5–7 cm) long and less than ½ in (1 cm) wide. The stiff, curved or pendulous axillary inflorescences, shorter than the leaves, bear 1–2 pretty white flowers measuring about ½ in (1 cm) across. The orchid usually flowers in spring-summer but also at other times of the year.
**Cultivation** This species is grown on cork or on a tree-fern raft where it grows easily and abundantly. Well tended specimens produce several inflorescences almost simultaneously and remain in bloom for many months. *T. formosanum* thrives in cool, moist surroundings if watered frequently so the substratum never dries out, especially in the hottest months. Well-developed specimens may throw out lateral shoots provided with a well-developed root system for the creation of new plants, which grow quite quickly.

## 150 THUNIA ALBA Rchb. f.
(Arethuseae, Thuniinae)

**Synonym** *Phaius albus* Wall.
**Origin** Burma, northern India.
**Description** Medium-large terrestrial plant. The pseudobulbs are fusiform, very thin and elongate, close together on the rhizome, generally 20–40 in (50–60 cm) tall, sometimes more than 3 ft (1 m), with leaves down to the base. These are alternate, oblong-lanceolate, pointed, horizontal, coriaceous, deciduous, those near the tip being about 6 in (16 cm) long, the lower ones shorter. The terminal inflorescence, pendulous and fairly lax, is made up of 5–10 white and purple flowers measuring 2–3 in (5–7 cm) across which do not open entirely and last about one week. The orchid flowers in late spring and summer.
**Cultivation** An easily grown plant that should be kept in a well-drained pot proportional to its size. The compost can be either osmunda fiber, bark mixed with sphagnum or even leafmold. Abundant and frequent watering should be stopped completely after the flowers drop and the leaves start to turn yellow, and regularly resumed only when the newly developing roots are a few inches long. This is also the best time to repot.

## 151 TRICHOCENTRUM FUSCUM Lindl.
(Cymbidieae, Oncidiinae)

**Origin** Brazil.
**Description** Small plant with practically no pseudobulbs and with a creeping, well-branched rhizome. The single leaves are coriaceous, lanceolate, about 4 in (10 cm) long and about ½ in (1 cm) wide. The pendulous flower stem bears several long-lasting flowers that open in succession; they are quite big in relation to the size of the plant, with olive-green petals and sepals and a white, bilobed lip equipped with a spur. The orchid flowers in autumn.
**Cultivation** This species, like the other 12 or so that belong to the genus, can be grown either on tree-fern rafts or in small pots; in the latter case the most frequently used potting media are osmunda fiber, tree-fern fiber or finely chopped bark. Watering should be sufficient to keep the mix constantly wet but not waterlogged, for this is very harmful to the plants, as is too little water which may quickly kill them. Repotting should be done only when absolutely necessary: the plants do not like to be disturbed.

## 152  TRICHOGLOTTIS SMITHII Carr
(Vandeae, Sarcanthinae)

**Origin** Borneo.

**Description** Medium-sized plant without pseudobulbs, monopodial in structure. The stem, 8–12 in (20–30 cm) long, is stiff, erect, and has aerial roots. The numerous alternate leaves, about ½ in (1 cm) apart, are coriaceous, linear-elliptic, unequally bilobed, 2½–3 in (6–8 cm) long and about ½ in (1.5 cm) wide. The very short axillary inflorescences are usually single-flowered. The flowers, about 1½ in (3 cm) in diameter, are quite showy, white with cinnamon spots and magenta on the lip, and long-lasting. The orchid generally flowers in the warmest months of the year.

**Cultivation** This species, like the 60 or so others belonging to the genus, is not widely cultivated. It is best grown in well-drained, medium-small pots with bark as the growing medium. Watering needs to be regular throughout the year. Repotting should be carried out only when the medium shows signs of breaking up. An extremely bright position and very humid surroundings are necessary for abundant flowering.

## 153  TRICHOPILIA SUAVIS Lindl. & Paxt.
(Cymbidieae, Oncidiinae)

**Synonym** *Trichopilia kienastiana* Rchb. f.

**Origin** Costa Rica.

**Description** Medium-small plant. The pseudobulbs, fairly rounded, very compressed, 1½–2½ in (4–7 cm) tall, have a single apical leaf that is elliptic-lanceolate, pointed, coriaceous but flexible, erect or curved, usually about 8 in (20 cm) long and 1½–2 in (4–5 cm) wide. The basal inflorescence, pendulous or curved, quite short, is formed of 2–5 very showy flowers, large in relation to the plant's size, long-lasting, white with spots and streaks that vary in color from pink to purple, intensity and dimension. The orchid flowers in early spring.

**Cultivation** This species, like many of the 30 or so others that constitute the genus, is quite commonly cultivated. It is usually grown in medium-small pots, using any type of well-drained mix that does not retain too much water. During the growth period watering should be regular, then stopped for several weeks. When resting, the plants should be kept in a cooler, well-ventilated position. Repotting should be done every year.

## 154 TRIDACTYLE TRIDACTYLITES (Rolfe) Schltr.
(Vandeae, Aerangidinae)

**Origin** Tropical Africa.

**Description** Medium-sized plant without pseudobulbs. The stiff, generally erect stem, 12–16 in (30–40 cm) long, bears coriaceous, horizontal, alternate, unequally bilobed leaves, set well apart, about 3 in (7 cm) in length. The inflorescences, usually short and averagely lax, are made up of a few flowers with a diameter of about ½ in (1 cm); they are greenish-white with a trilobed lip and a spur about ¼ in (7 mm) long. The orchid flowers in spring.

**Cultivation** This species, like the others belonging to the same genus, is rather rare in collections. It can be grown either on a piece of wood or in medium-small pots with well-drained medium. Watering, plentiful and frequent during the growth period, should be stopped until new plant growth commences. These plants do not like to be disturbed and repotting is advisable only when the compost, beginning to break up, retains too much water.

---

## 155 TRIGONIDIUM OBTUSUM Lindl.
(Maxillarieae, Maxillariinae)

**Origin** Brazil, Guayana.

**Description** Medium-sized plant. The pseudobulbs are ovoid, compressed, close together on the rhizome, roughening with age, about 2 in (5 cm) tall, enfolded at the base by several dry bracts and furnished with 2 apical leaves that are linear-lanceolate, pointed, coriaceous, 8–20 in (20–50 cm) long and 1½ in (3–4 cm) wide. The numerous stiff, erect, basal flower stems, about 6 in (15 cm) in length, bear a single campanulate, long-lasting, variably colored flower, generally a mixture of white and yellow. This species is very similar to *T. egertonianum* Batem., but differs in not having a distinctly warty callus on the lower side of the apex of the lip. The orchid normally flowers in spring.

**Cultivation** The species that belong to this genus are not commonly cultivated, despite the fact that they are not very difficult to grow. This one should be raised in a pot proportional to its size, and it adapts to any kind of potting medium. Abundant watering during the growth period needs to be reduced afterwards so that the mix can dry out between applications. The plants should be repotted and divided only when well developed.

## 156 VANDA Jones
(Vandeae, Sarcanthinae)

**Origin** Australia, Philippines, northern India, Indonesia, Indochinese peninsula, Sri Lanka, Taiwan.

**Description** Medium and large plants without pseudobulbs, monopodial in structure. The stiff, generally erect stem is in some species 8–12 in (20–30 cm) long: *V. cristata* Lindl., *V. parviflora* Lindl., *V. coerulescens* Griff.; in others it may easily extend to 6½ ft (2 m): *V. teres* Lindl., *V. tricolor* Lindl., *V. spathulata* Spreng. In certain species the long, branched and often very thick roots grow abundantly, even along the stem, forming an inextricable tangle. The morphology of the leaves is the basis for distinguishing two groups: the larger group displays ribbon-like leaves, curved, coriaceous, fairly close together, with an unequally bilobed apex; the other has cylindrical, pointed, fairly well spaced leaves. The inflorescences, produced at the leaf axil, are erect or curved, made up of a few flowers, as in *V. cristata*, or many, as in the majority of other species. The flowers, which vary considerably in shape, size and color, are showy, very long-lasting and open in succession. The flowering period varies according to species; some bloom once a year, others twice, and almost all produce 2 or more inflorescences.

**Cultivation** Most of the species that belong to the genus *Vanda* require hothouse treatment; but some, e.g. *V. coerulea* Lindl. need lower temperatures, especially at night, and are therefore better suited to the temperate greenhouse. As a rule *Vanda* orchids are grown in baskets that vary in dimension according to the plant size, with or without pieces of charcoal, crocks or bark; but they can also be cultivated in pots proportional to the spread of their roots, filled with reasonably sized pieces of the above-mentioned materials. These orchids should not be repotted too often. The thick roots, when split or cut off, may easily rot, and in order to produce plenty of flowers the plants must have a well-developed root system. When a plant becomes too tall or sheds its lower leaves, it is advisable to divide it in two. The apical portion, with several roots, preferably not too long, can be potted (take care not to damage the roots themselves); the basal section can be kept in the old container where, with a few months of normal attention, it will send out lateral shoots which, once sufficiently developed, can be divided. In the course of repotting, it is a good idea to immerse the roots for a few minutes in clean water so as to make them flexible and avoid the risk of breaking them. In the case of plants grown in baskets, since it is impossible to remove them without damaging the root system, it is best, when repotting, to insert them into a bigger basket after getting rid of the dead roots. The stem of the *Vanda* species should be attached to a support, particularly after repotting, to provide greater stability. Furthermore it is advisable to keep basket specimens suspended rather than to rest them on tables or shelves; this prevents the rapidly growing and numerous roots from sticking to

Above left: *Vanda tricolor* Lindl. var. *suavis* (Lindl.) Veitch.
Above right: *Vanda teres* Lindl.
Below left: *Vanda coerulea* Lindl.
Below right: *Vanda lamellata* Lindl.

surfaces. Watering should be regular throughout the year; during the hottest months, especially in the case of basket plants, frequent spraying with water is highly beneficial. The majority of these plants thrive in very bright light, although direct sunlight is likely to scorch the leaves and some form of shading or tinted glass is necessary. In their countries of origin *Vanda* species with cylindrical leaves are nevertheless grown in full sun with excellent results.

**Hybrids** The genus *Vanda*, with some 40 species, has been widely used for hybridization, sometimes in conjunction with related genera of subtribe Sarcanthinae. Hybrids thus obtained often display flowers of such lovely colors and tones, and of such long duration that they have become very much sought by collectors and florists alike. The genera most frequently employed in crosses with *Vanda* species are: *Euanthe, Ascocentrum, Arachnis, Renanthera, Aerides* and *Phalaenopsis*.

*Vanda sanderiana* Rchb. f. was transferred by Schlechter to the genus *Euanthe* in 1914, and therefore the *Vanda* hybrids listed among the parents of this species with extremely beautiful flowers are nowadays called *Vandanthe,* a typical example being *Vandanthe* Rothschildiana (*V. coerulea* × *Euanthe sanderiana*).

Below: *Vanda* Kultana Gold × *V.* Rasri AM
Opposite above: *Vandanthe* Rothschildiana
Opposite below: *Vandanthe* Patricia Low

## 157 VANDOPSIS PARISHII (Veitch ex Rchb. f.) Schltr.
(Vandeae, Sarcanthinae)

**Synonym** *Vanda parishii* Veitch ex Rchb. f.
**Origin** Burma, Thailand.
**Description** Medium-sized plant without pseudobulbs, monopodial in structure. The stem is erect, generally 4–8 in (10–20 cm) high, sheathed by the base of the leaves. The carinate leaves are opposite, close together, elliptic-oblong, unequally bilobed at the apex, very coriaceous, light green, 6–10 in (15–25 cm) long and 1½–3 in (4–7 cm) wide. The axillary inflorescence, stiff, erect or curved, lax, is made up of not more than 6–7 yellow flowers with reddish-brown markings and a diameter of about 2 in (5 cm), very conspicuous and long-lasting. The variety *mariottianum* Rchb. f. has flowers that are more rounded, with deeper colors. The orchid usually flowers in summer.

**Cultivation** This species, like the other 8 or so species belonging to the genus, is a sturdy plant of slow growth; it is cultivated in baskets or in pots proportional to its size, with any type of potting medium. Watering needs to be regular all through the year. In their countries of origin these orchids are often grown outdoors in full sunlight; under glass they are best kept in a bright position with some shade. Repotting should be carried out only when the compost starts to break up.

## 158 VANILLA IMPERIALIS Krzl.
(Vanilleae, Vanillinae)

**Origin** Tropical Africa.
**Description** Plants that resemble lianas, without pseudobulbs. The stem is cylindrical, many meters long, with a diameter of 1 in (2–3 cm) and internodes measuring 5–6 in (12–15 cm) in length. The leaves are elliptic, fleshy, one per node, about 6 in (15 cm) long and 2½–3 in (6–8 cm) wide. From opposite the leaves, one or more fairly thick and very long aerial roots arise. The dense, apical inflorescence consists of numerous showy green and purple flowers that open in succession, do not last long (1–2 days) and measure about 4 in (10 cm) in diameter. The same inflorescence may produce flowers for several years, becoming gradually longer each season. The orchid flowers in summer.

**Cultivation** Easily cultivated plant that requires plenty of room because the liana-like stem grows and branches rapidly. Given the large number of aerial roots, the pots in which the plants grow should not be too big in relation to the overall plant size. The stems can be twined around a supporting stake or trained freely over a trellis. In order to bloom, these plants have to reach a considerable size. Regular watering is necessary throughout the year. The three main species used for the commercial production of vanilla flavorings are *V. planifolia* G. Jackson, *V. pompona* Schiede and *V. tahitensis* J.W. Moore.

## 159 XYLOBIUM VARIEGATUM (Ruiz & Pavon) Garay & Dunsterville
(Maxillarieae, Bifrenariinae)

**Synonym** *Xylobium squalens* (Lindle.) Lindl.
**Origin** Costa Rica to Brazil.
**Description** Medium-sized plant. The pseudobulbs, 2–3 in (5–8 cm) tall, are ovoid, rugose, and situated close together on the rhizome. The leaves, usually 2, rarely 3, are apical, elliptic-oblong, plicate, membranous, with a short stalk, and are 16–20 in (40–50 cm) long and about 3 in (8 cm) wide. The dense basal inflorescence, curved or erect, 4–6 in (10–15 cm) long, is composed of numerous small, pink flowers flushed with maroon, of long duration. The orchid flowers several times a year, most freely in summer.
**Cultivation** An easily cultivated plant that is generally grown in medium-small pots with any kind of well-drained potting medium. Watering should be regular and plentiful during the growth period and afterwards reduced so that the medium dries out between successive applications. Specimens should be allowed to increase in order to produce more and better flowers. Repotting should be carried out when the compost starts to break up.

## 160 ZOOTROPHION ATROPURPUREUM
(Lindl.) Luer
(Epidendreae, Pleurothallidinae)

**Synonym** *Cryptophoranthus atropurpureus* (Lindl.) Rolfe.
**Origin** Costa Rica, Cuba, Jamaica.
**Description** Small plant without pseudobulbs, with a slender branching rhizome. The stems, thin, erect, very close together and enfolded by dry bracts, bear a single apical leaf, coriaceous, elliptic-obovate, with a short stalk, about 3½ in (9 cm) long and 1 in (2–3 cm) wide. The flower stem, which sprouts from the base of the leaves, is quite short and bears a single flower of characteristic shape, in varying tones of crimson. The orchid generally flowers between late summer and early winter.
**Cultivation** This species is grown on a tree-fern raft or in small pots, with a potting mix consisting of finely chopped bark and sphagnum. Watering should be sufficient to keep the medium constantly moist, but not soaked, as this may give rise to root rot. Repotting should be done only when the compost starts to break up.

## 161 ZYGOPETALUM INTERMEDIUM Lindl.
(Maxillarieae, Zygopetalinae)

**Synonym** *Zygopetalum mackayi* Paxt. non Hooker.
**Origin** Bolivia, Brazil, Peru.
**Description** Large plant. The pseudobulbs are conical-ovoid, about 3 in (8 cm) tall, close together on the rhizome, longitudinally furrowed with age. The 3–5 leaves are apical, elliptic-lanceolate, pointed, coriaceous but flexible, 8–24 in (20–60 cm) long and about 2½ in (6 cm) wide. The stiff, erect, lax inflorescence, 20–24 in (50–60 cm) long, is made up of 5–8 large showy flowers. These are essentially green, brown and blue. They are showy and long-lasting, and give out a very strong scent similar to that of jonquils. *Z. intermedium* is often confused with *Z. mackayi* Hooker, the main difference being that its lip is downy. The orchid flowers in autumn and winter.
**Cultivation** This species is probably more widely cultivated than any other of the genus. The plants are easy to grow in medium-large pots, where they increase readily. Bark is the growing medium most frequently used. Watering should be regular all through the year. Repotting and division present no problems but are best carried out when the plants are large in order to guarantee a continuity of flowers.

---

## 162 ZYGOPETALUM MAXILLARE Lodd.
(Maxillarieae, Zygopetalinae)

**Synonym** *Zygopetalum mandibulare* Rchb. f.
**Origin** Brazil, Paraguay.
**Description** Medium-small plant. The pseudobulbs are fairly small, ovoid-elongate, compressed, rugose, about 1½ in (4 cm) tall, spaced apart on the rhizome. The 5–6 leaves are apical, narrowly lanceolate, coriaceous but flexible, about 12 in (30 cm) long and about 1 in (2 cm) wide. The basal inflorescence is stiff, erect or curved, lax, normally 6–8 in (15–20 cm) but sometimes up to 12 in (30 cm) long. It is made up of 5–8 showy, greenish-brown and purple long-lasting flowers, measuring 1 in (2–3 cm) across. The orchid flowers in winter and spring.
**Cultivation** This species is not common in collections; it is grown in small pots or on a tree-fern raft. The recommended growing medium is tree-fern fiber or a mixture of finely chopped bark, osmunda fiber and sphagnum, which should be kept moist. The plants are delicate and need to be handled carefully.
**Hybrids** Various species of the genus *Zygopetalum* have been crossed to obtain very beautiful clones which nowadays can be purchased easily; it has also been hybridized with various species of related genera such as *Batemania, (Zygobatemania), Colax (Zygocolax), Aganisia (Zygonisia),* but these hybrids, although interesting, are not generally available.

# GLOSSARY

**anther** the pollen-bearing part of the stamen of the flower.

**apex** the tip (of a stem or pseudobulb).

**apical** used to describe the inflorescence when this is produced at the apex of the stem or pseudobulb.

**axil** the angle between the upper side of a leaf or stem and the supporting stem.

**axillary** used to describe the inflorescence when this grows from the leaf axil.

**basal** used to describe the inflorescence when this is produced from the base of the pseudobulb.

**bilobed** (of leaves) divided into two lobes.

**bract** a specialized leaf or leaflike part usually situated at the base of a flower or inflorescence.

**bracteate** having bracts.

**caducous** generally used to describe leaves that last only one season.

**calcareous** (of soil) chalky.

**callus** the thickened part of the lip.

**campanulate** bell-shaped; used to describe a flower that does not open fully.

**carinate** (of leaves) having a longitudinal ridge.

**carpels** elements that join together to form the outer casing of the ovary; in orchids there are always three.

**clavate** club-shaped.

**column** the columnlike structure in the orchid flower composed of the united stamens and style.

**coriaceous** (of leaves) leathery.

**deciduous** shedding the leaves annually.

**distichous** (of leaves) arranged alternately in two vertical rows on opposite sides of the stem.

**elliptic** having the form of an ellipse.

**epichile** the tip of the elaborate lip of the flowers of certain genera such as *Stanhopea*.

**epiphyte, epiphytic** used to describe a plant that grows above the ground supported nonparasitically by another plant or object, deriving its nutrients from the surrounding air.

**falcate** curved like a scythe or sickle.

**fusiform** spindle-shaped; rounded and tapering from the middle toward each end.

**globose** having the shape of a globe; more or less spherical.

**hypochile** the basal section of the lip of the flowers of genera such as *Stanhopea*.

**imbricate** (of leaves) when the top of the lower leaf overlaps the bottom of the upper leaf.

**lanceolate** (of leaves) narrow and tapering toward the apex.

**lax** used to describe an inflorescence where the flowers are spaced well apart from each other.

**ligulate** (of leaves) ribbon-shaped; sheathing the stem.

**linear** narrow and elongated.

**lithophyte, lithophytic** used to describe a plant that grows on the surface of rocks.

**mesochile** the middle section of the lip of the flowers of certain genera such as *Stanhopea*.

**monopodial** an orchid plant that has neither rhizome nor pseudobulbs (see **sympodial**).

**oblanceolate** (of leaves) narrow and tapering at the base, but broadening out toward the apex.

**obovate** (of leaves) having an oval shape with the narrowest part at the base (see page 16).

**opposite** (of leaves) a pair of leaves from each node, one on either side of the stem.

**osmunda fiber** a common growing medium used in the cultivation of orchids. It consists of the roots of the fern *Osmunda regalis*.

**ovoid** egg-shaped; having the solid shape of an egg.

**pendulous** (of an inflorescence) hanging down loosely.

**persistent** used to describe leaves that stay on the plant for more than one growing season and fall only after a few years.

**petal** floral leaves that together make up the corolla.

**petiolate** used to describe leaves that have stalks.

**plicate** folded like a fan.

**pruinose** covered with a frostlike bloom or powdery secretion, as a plant surface.

**pseudobulb** part of the stem transformed into a reserve organ.

**pubescent** covered with soft, fine hairs.

**pyriform** pear-shaped.

**rachis** the stem of an inflorescence when this is somewhat elongated as in a raceme.

**rhizome** an underground stem which acts as a storage organ.

**rugose** wrinkled.

**rupicolous** growing amongst rocks.

**sepal** a leaf-like segment of the calyx, making up the outer layer whorl of the flower.

**sessile** without a stalk or stem.

**sphagnum** moss of the genus *Sphagnum* frequently used as a growing medium for many orchid genera.

**stellate** starlike.

**subterminal** used to describe an inflorescence that occurs below the apex.

**sympodial** plants having a rhizome and pseudobulbs (see **monopodial**).

**terminal** used to describe an inflorescence that occurs at the tip of the stem.

**trilobed** with three lobes.

**tree-fern fiber** a fibrous growing medium obtained from various species of *Dicksonia*.

**umbel** an inflorescence in which the flowers are borne on short stalks that spring from a common stem all reaching the same length.

**undulate** wavy.

**velamen** spongy tissue that surrounds the roots.

# BIBLIOGRAPHY

Bechtel, H., Cribb, P., and Launert, E., *The Manual of Cultivated Orchid Species*, Blandford Press, Poole, Dorset, U.K., 1981

Correll, D.S., *Native Orchids of North America, North Mexico,* Stanford University Press, U.S.A., 1978

Cribb, P., *The Genus Paphiopedilum*, Collingridge, London, U.K., 1987

Curtis, C.H., *Orchids. Their Description and Cultivation*, Putnam & Co. Ltd., London, U.K., 1950

Dressler, R.L., *The Orchids. Natural History and Classification*, Harvard University Press, Cambridge, U.S.A., 1981

Holttum, R.E., *Orchids of Malaya* (in *A Revised Flora of Malaya* 3rd eition), Government Printing Office, Singapore, 1964

Hawkes, A.D., *Encyclopedia of Cultivated Orchids*, Faber and Faber Ltd., London, U.K., 1965

McKenzie Black, P., *Beautiful Orchids*, Hamlyn Publishing Group, London, U.K., 1973

Noble, M., *You Can Grow Cattleya Orchids*, Mary Noble, Jacksonville, U.S.A., 1968

  *You Can Grow Phalaenopsis Orchids*, Mary Noble, Jacksonville, U.S.A., 1971

  *You Can Grow Orchids* (4th edition), Mary Noble, Jacksonville, U.S.A., 1975

Rossi, W., and Bassani, P., *Orchidee spontanee del Lazio*, Edizioni Coopsit, Italy, 1985

Sbrana, G., *Le Orchidee* Edagricole, Bologna, Italy, 1975

Sweeth, H.R., *The Genus Phalaenopsis*, Day Printing Corp., Pomona, California, U.S.A., 1980

Tyson, Northen, R., *Home Orchid Growing* (3rd edition), Van Nostrand Reinhold Co., New York, U.S.A., 1970

  *Miniature Orchids,* Van Nostrand Reinhold Co., New York, U.S.A., 1980

William, L.O., and Allen, P.H., *Orchidaceae. Flora of Panama, Annals of Missouri Botanical Garden*, 1946-1949

Williams, J.G., and Williams, A.E., *Field Guide to Orchids of North America*, Universe Books, New York, U.S.A., 1983

Williams, J.G., Williams, A.E., and Arlott, N., *Guide des Orchidées sauvages d'Europe et du Bassin méditerranéen*, Delachaux et Niestlé, Neuchâtel-Paris, France, 1979

Withner, C. (ed.), *The Orchids. A Scientific Survey*, The Ronald Press Company, New York, U.S.A., 1959

The national orchid societies in several countries of the world publish their own bulletins. The three listed here below were consulted during the preparation of this book:

Federal Republic of Germany: *Die Orchidee*, D.O.G., D-2724 Sottrum, Arndtstrasse 8.

Great Britain: *Orchid Review*, Orchid Review Ltd., Katukelle House, Victoria Village, Trinity, Jersey, Channel Islands.

United States: *American Orchid Society Bulletin*, 6000 South Olive Avenue, West Palm Beach, Florida 33405

# INDEX

The numbers refer to the entries;
when these are in italic this indicates
an illustration.
(s) denotes a synonym.

Acacallis cyanea 1
Acineta superba 2
Aerangis luteo-alba 3
Aëranthus sesquipedale (s) 7
Aerides
    fieldingii (s) 4
    japonicum (s) 141
    rosea 4
    williamsii (s) 4
Aëridopsis 120
Aganisia
    coerulea (s) 1
    tricolor (s) 1
Ancistrochilus rothschildianus 5
Angraecum
    caudatum (s) 124
    distichum 6
    falcatum (s) 97
    mirabile (s) 3
    rhodostictum (s) 3
    sesquipedale 7
    Veitchii 7
Anguloa
    clowesii 8
    superba (s) 2
Angulocaste 85
Ansellia
    africana 9
    africana var. nilotica (s) 9
    gigantea (s) 9
Arachnanthe clarkei (s) 63
Arachnis 10
    clarkei (s) 63
    Maggie Oei 10
Arachnopsis 120
Aranthera 131
Ascocenda
    Suk Sumran Beauty 11
    Yip Sum Wah 11
Ascocentrum 11
    curvifolium 11
    miniatum 11
Ascofinetia 11
Asconopsis 11, 120

Aspasia
    epidendroides 12
    fragrans (s) 12
Barkeria spectabilis 13
Batemania burtii (s) 70
Bifrenaria
    hadwenii (s) 140
    tetragona 14
Blc. Autumn Glow 'Green Goddess' 27
Blc. Malworth 'Orchidglade' 27
Bletia angustata (s) 145
Bletilla striata 15
Bolusiella talbotii 16
Bothriochilus bellus (s) 31
Brapasia
Brassavola
    digbyana (s) 133
    nodosa 17
    venosa (s) 17
Brassia
    aristata (s) 18
    brachiata (s) 18
    verrucosa 18
Broughtonia
    coccinea (s) 19
    sanguinea 19
Bulbophyllum
    falcatum 20
    lepidum 21
    lobbii 22
Calanthe
    triplicata 23
    veratrifolia (s) 23
Catasetum
    barbatum 24
    bungerothii (s) 26
    fimbriatum 25
    pileatum 26
    proboscideum (s) 24
    spinosum (s) 24
Cattleya 27
    araguaiensis 27
    aurantiaca 27
    bowringiana 27

lutea (s) 74
  superbiens (s) 139
  warscewiczii var. gigas 27
Cattleytonia 19
  Keith Roth 'Roma' 19
Chondrorhyncha discolor (s) 29
Cirrhaea
  dependens 28
  fuscolutea (s) 28
Cirrhopetalum gamosepalum (s) 21
Cochleanthes discolor 29
Cochlioda noezliana 30
Coelia bella 31
Coelogyne
  cristata 32
  densiflora (s) 33
  maculata (s) 125
  massangeana 33
  pandurata 34
Colax jugosus (s) 116
Colmanara 101
Comparettia
  falcata 35
  rosea (s) 35
Coryanthes speciosa 36
Cryptophoranthus atropurpureus
  (s) 160
Cycnoches 95
  haagii 37
  versicolor (s) 37
Cymbidium 38
  Alexanderi 'Westonbirt' 38
  Cariga 'Canary' 38
  dependens (s) 28
  eburneum 38
  eburneum-lowianum 38
  Jugfrau 'Dos Pueblos' 38
  Lillian Stewart 'St. Sherrie' 38
  lowianum 38
  miniature Silvia Miller 'Paola' 38
  San Francisco 'Stephenson' 38
  speciosissimum (s) 32
  suavissimum 38
  tracyanum 38
Cypripedium
  calceolus 39
  flavescens (s) 39
  luteum (s) 39
  pubescens (s) 39
  schlimii (s) 123
Dendrobium
  aggregatum 40
  antennatum 41
  cebolleta (s) 103
  chrysotoxum 42
  cucumerinum 43
  hyacinthoides (s) 62
  ferox (s) 44
  jenkinsii 40

  lindleyi 40
  macrophyllum 44
  nobile 45
  nobile var. pendulum 45
  parishii 46
  senile 47
  stratiotes 41
  suavissimum (s) 42
  Utopia 'Messenger' 45
  veitchianum (s) 44
Dendrochilum glumaceum 48
Disa
  barellii (s) 49
  grandiflora (s) 49
  uniflora 49
Doritaenopsis 50, 120
Doritis
  buyssoniana 50
  pulcherrima 50
Dracula erythrochaete 51
Dryadella zebrina 52
Encyclia
  cochleata 53
  maculosa 54
  mariae 55
  vitellina 56
Epidendrum
  ciliare 57
  clavatum (s) 61
  cochleatum (s) 53
  cristatum 58
  fulgens (s) 59
  ibaguense 59
  maculosum (s) 54
  nodosum (s) 17
  parkinsonianum 60
  purparescens 61
  raniferum (s) 58
  radicans (s) 59
  sanguineum (s) 19
  spectabile (s) 13
  utricularioides (s) 71
  vitellinum (s) 71
Epiphronitis Veitchii 59
Eria hyacinthoides 62
Esmeralda clarkei 63
Eulophia guineensis 64
Eulophidium maculatum (s) 102
Fergusonara 27
Galeandra baueri 65
Gastocalanthe 23
Gastrochilus bellinus 66
Gomesa recurva 67
Gongora
  donckelaariana (s) 68
  truncata 68
  viridipurpurea (s) 28
Haemaria discolor (s) 83
Hartwegia purpurea (s) 96

Helcia sanguinolenta 69
Huntleya
    cerina (s) 118
    meleagris 70
Ionopsis
    paniculata (s) 71
    utricularioides 71
Jumellea sagittata 72
Kingidium deliciosum 73
Kingiella decumbens (s) 73
Laelia
    flava 74
    fulva (s) 74
    gouldiana 75
    grandis 76
    jongheana 77
    superbiens (s) 139
Lc. Butterfly Bell 'Queen of Formosa'
    27
Lemboglossum
    cervantesii 78
    maculatum 100
Lepanthes ovalis 79
Leptotes bicolor 80
Limodorum striatum 15
Liparis guineensis 81
Lockartia lunifera 82
Ludisia discolor 83
Lycaste
    aromatica 84
    deppei 85
    suaveolens (s) 84
Lycasteria 85
Lyfrenaria 14
Macradenia multiflora 86
Malaxis latifolia 87
Masdevallia
    astata (s) 51
    erythrochaete (s) 51
    glandulosa 88
    ignea 89
    Marguerite 90
    militaris (s) 89
    triangularis 90
    zebrina (s) 52
Maxillaria
    acutifolia (s) 93
    aromatica (s) 84
    deppei (s) 85
    fuscata (s) 92
    jugosa (s) 116
    picta 92
    rufescens 93
    tetragona (s) 14
    xanthina (s) 129
Megaclinium falcatum (s) 20
Microstylis latifolia (s) 87
Miltonia 94
    regnellii 94

Charlesworthii 94
Miltoniopsis 94
Mormodes
    histrio (s) 95
    warscewiczii 95
Mystacidium distichum (s) 6
Nageliella purpurea 96
Neofinetia falcata 97
Notylia
    barkeri 98
    bipartita (s) 98
    trisepala (s) 98
Odontocidium Tiger Hambühren 101
Odontoglossum
    alexandrae (s) 99
    cervantesii (s) 78
    crispum 99
    grande (s) 137
    maculatum 100
    membranaceum (s) 78
    cervantesii (s) 78
    noezlianum 30
Odontonia 101
Oeceoclades maculata 102
Oncidium
    cebolleta 103
    crispum 105
    equitants 110
    fimbriatum 104
    flabelliferum (s) 105
    forbesii 105
    gardneri 105
    guttatum (s) 106
    luridum 106
    macropetalum 107
    marshallianum 105
    massangei (s) 111
    Misty Pink × O. pulchellum 110
    onustum 108
    ornithorhynchum 109
    pulchellum 110
    rogersii 112
    sphacelatum 111
    varicosum 112
    verrucosum (s) 18
Ophrys bombyliflora 113
Orchis militaris 114
Ornithocephalus
    elephas (s) 115
    inflexus 115
Pabstia jugosa 116
Paphiopedilum 117
    armeniacum 117
    bellatulum 117
    Brachypetalum 117
    callosum 117
    charlesworthii 117
    concolor 117
    delenatii 117

*druryi* 117
  *emersonii* 117
  *fairrieanum* 117
  *godefroyae* 117
  *haynaldianum* 117
  'Westonbirt' *117*
  *hirsutissimum* 117
  *insigne* 117
  *liemianum* 117
  *lowii* 117
  *malipoense* 117
  *micranthum* 117
  *niveum* 117
  *parishii* 117
  *philippinense* 117
  *rothschildianum* 117
  *sanderianum* 117
  *schlimii* (s) *123*
  *spicerianum* 117
  *sukhakulii* 117
  *venustum* 117
  *victoriaregina* 117
  *villosum* 117
  Winston Churchill 'Indomitable' *117*
*Peristeria humboldtii* (s) 2
*Pescatorea*
  *cerina* 118
  *lehmannii* 119
*Phaiocalanthe* 23
*Phaius albus* (s) *150*
*Phalaenopsis* 120
  *amabilis* 120
  *amboinensis* 120
  Antarctic 120
  Antonio Carnana 'Roma' *120*
  *cornu-cervi* 120
  *deliciosa* (s) *73*
  Elisabethae 120
  *esmeralda* (s) *50*
  Estrella Rojo × George Vasquez
    *120*
  *gigantea* 120
  *lueddemanniana* 120
  *mannii* 120
  *parishii* 120
  Redfan 'Grazia' *120*
  *remestadiana* 120
  *sanderiana* 120
  *schilleriana* 120
  *stuartiana* 120
  Vallauris × *P. fuscata 120*
  *violacea* 120
  *violacea* (Borneo form) *120*
  *violacea* (Malaysian form) *120*
*Phalandopsis* 120
*Pholidota*
  *articulata* 121
  *decurva* (s) *121*
*Phragmipedium*

Dominianum 122
Grande 122
*pearcei* 122
*schlimii* 123
Schroderae 122
Sedenii 122
*Plectrelminthus caudatus 124*
*Pleione maculata 125*
*Pleurothallis*
  *ospinae* (s) *133*
  *pterophora* 126
*Polystachya*
  *affinis* 127
  *bella* 128
*Promenaea*
  *citrina* (s) 129
  *xanthina* 129
*Renantanda*
*Renanthera*
  *imschootiana* 130
  *monachica* 131
*Renanthopsis* 120, 131
*Restrepia antennifera* 132
*Rhyncholaelia digbyana 133*
*Rhynchostylis gigantea 134*
*Rodriguezia*
  *bracteata* 135
  *recurva* (s) *67*
*Rodrigueziella gomezoides 136*
*Rossioglossum grande 137*
*Rothara* 27
*Saccolabium*
  *bellinum* (s) *66*
  *giganteum* (s) *134*
*Sanderara* 101
*Sarcochilus*
  *hartmannii* 138
  *rubicentrum* (s) *138*
*Satyrium grandiflorum* (s) *49*
*Schomburgkia superbiens 138*
*Scuticaria hadwenii 140*
*Sedirea japonica 141*
*Selenipedium*
  *pearcei* (s) *122*
  *schlimii* (s) *123*
*Sobralia macrantha 142*
*Sophronitella violacea 143*
*Sophronitis*
  *coccinea* 144
  *grandiflora* (s) *144*
  *violacea* (s) *143*
*Spathoglottis*
  *lilacina* (s) *145*
  *plicata 145*
*Spiranthes* 146
  *spiralis* 146
*Stanhopea* 147
  Assidensis 147
  Bellaerensis 147

bucephalus (s) *147*
expansa (s) *147*
guttata (s) *147*
insignis *147*
jenischiana *147*
marshii (s) *147*
Mem. Paul Allen 147
oculata *147*
radiosa (s) *147*
tigrina *147*
Stelis 148
argentata *148*
ciliaris *148*
Tetramicra bicolor (s) *80*
Theodorea gomezoides (s) *136*
Thrixpermum formosanum *149*
Thunia alba *150*
Trichocentrum fuscum *151*
Trichoglottis smithii *152*
Trichopilia
kienastiana (s) *153*
suavis *153*
Tridactyle tridactylites *154*
Trigonidium obtusum *155*
Vanda 156
coerulea *156*
coerulescens *156*
cristata *156*
Kultana Gold × V. Rasri *156*
lamellata *156*
parishii (s) *157*
parviflora *156*
sanderiana *156*

spathulata *156*
teres *156*
tricolor *156*
tricolor var. suavis *156*
Vandaenopsis 120
Vandanthe
Patricia *156*
Rothschildiana *156*
Vandopsis parishii *157*
Vanilla
imperialis *158*
planifolia *158*
pompona *158*
tahitensis *158*
Vuylstekeara 101
Warrea discolor (s) *29*
Wilsonara 101
Xylobium
squalens (s) *159*
variegatum *159*
Zootrophion atropurpureum *160*
Zygobatemania 162
Zygocaste (h) *85*
Zygocolax 162
Zygonisia 162
Zygopetalum
cerinum (s) *118*
intermedium *161*
lehmannii (s) *119*
mackayi (s) *161*
mandibulare (s) *162*
maxillare *162*
meleagris (s) *70*

## ACKNOWLEDGMENTS

Alberto Fanfani and Walter Rossi would like to thank all the friends who, by kindly granting access to their plants, made this book possible.

E. Bergonzo (Rome) 17, 38a, 45a, 46, 66, 67, 74, 84, 87, 105, 116, 125, 130, 134, 137, 147a, 149, p.246; D. Bitetti (Rome) p.33, 98, 135; G. Carava' (Varese) 48; A. Corvi (Varese) 2, 23, 65, 118, 133, 152,; M. Dalla Rosa (Rome) 29, 40, 43, 47, 55, 88, 90, 91, 96, 109, 117a-b-c-e-l, 120 a-d, 129, 138: Z. Fiorentini (Rome) 120 e-m, 157; G. Giorgi (Lavagna/Genoa) p.21, 45b; H. Mayer (Nairobi) 3, 27b, 128; F. Pugliese (Rome) p.24, p.25a, p.31, 8, 11b, 12, 22, 24b, 27d, 31, 34, 35, 42, 69, 71, 76, 77 80, 89, 95, 110a, 126, 136, 144, 147b, 148a, 150, 154, 162; C. Ravanello (Genoa) p.8/9; Royal Botanic Gardens (Kew, Great Britain) p.19, 21, 38c, 41, 44, 49, 54, 56, 63, 78, 79, 94, 115, 117f, 146a, 147e, 148b, 151, 153; Servizio Giardini del Comune di Roma p.40, p.41b, 27f, 117i, 156e,

Pictures not listed above come from Alberto Fanfani's collection or have been photographed from nature.